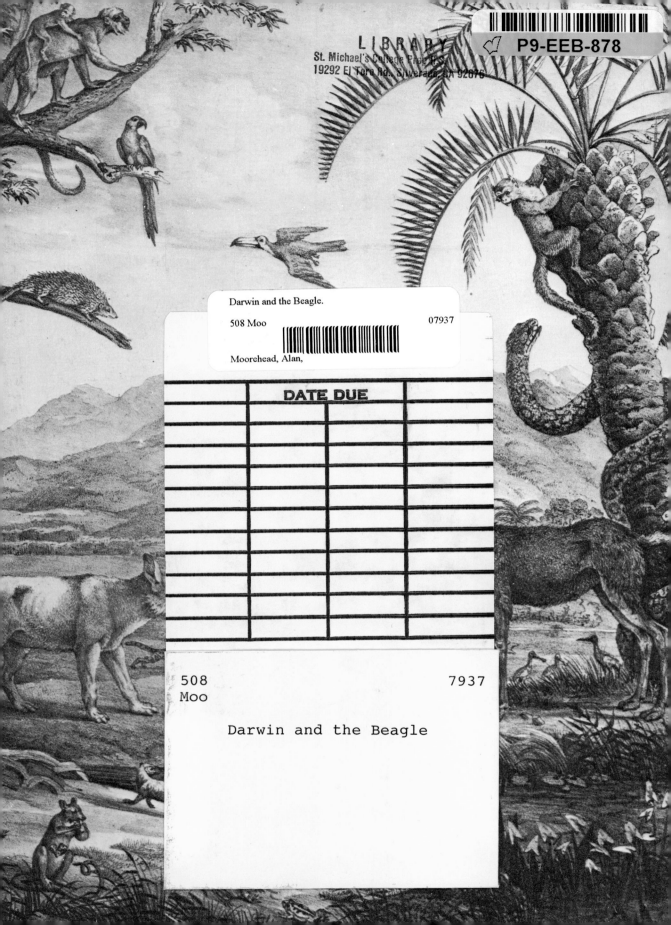

DARWIN AND THE BEAGLE

DARWIN AND THE BEAGLE

ALAN MOOREHEAD

HARPER & ROW, PUBLISHERS
NEW YORK & EVANSTON

Second Impression 1969
Third Impression 1969
Fourth Impression 1970
Fifth Impression 1970
Sixth Impression 1970
Seventh Impression 1970

This book was designed and produced by
George Rainbird Ltd
Marble Arch House, 44 Edgware Road, London w.2, England

House Editor: Enid Gordon
Designer: Ronald Clark
Index: Edward Howe
Maps: Tom Stalker-Miller

Filmset in Monophoto Imprint by
Jolly & Barber Ltd, Rugby
Color printed by Westerham Press Ltd, Kent
Text printed and bound by
Jarrold & Sons Ltd, Norwich

Library of Congress Catalog Card Number 69–17879

Printed in Great Britain for
Harper & Row, Publishers, Incorporated

A substantial portion of the
contents of this book appeared
originally in *The New Yorker*.

CONTENTS

ACKNOWLEDGMENTS

This book, parts of which were written in collaboration with my wife, was developed from an original film treatment which I wrote for Mr Robert Radnitz.

I would like to thank Mr James Fisher for his kindness in reading and correcting the manuscript, and the Royal Geographical Society for their generous assistance with the illustrations.

ALAN MOOREHEAD

Commissioned photographs for this book have been taken by the following photographers:

Derrick Witty: pages 23, 24, 73, 74 (above), 118–9, 120, 140, 149 (above), 159, 162, 171 (below), 209, 222, 242–3, 253, 254, 271, 272; 21 (right), 28, 29, 32, 34, 39, 40, 43, 44, 46, 49, 50, 51, 57, 58–9, 60, 63 (below right), 66, 68–9, 76, 81, 84, 85, 87, 95, 97, 98, 101, 102, 104, 108, 109, 111 (left), 112 (below), 122, 130, 133, 136, 142, 143, 144, 154, 156, 165, 168, 175, 176–7, 179, 185, 186, 189, 190, 194, 203 (below), 204 (below), 206–7, 212, 214, 216 (above), 227, 236–7, 245, 246, 249, 250–1, 256, 257, 265, 268, 269, 270, endpapers.

John Freeman: pages 53, 71, 72, 74 (below), 91, 92, 117, 137, 138–9, 149 (below), 150, 160–1, 171 (above), 172, 197, 200, 210, 219, 232, 241, 244; 63 (above, below left), 64, 65, 75, 78, 111 (right), 112 (above), 114, 115, 125, 126, 129, 146, 147, 152, 153, 164, 166, 178, 181, 184, 195, 203 (above), 204 (above), 213, 216 (below), 217, 225, 229, 233, 235, 238, 239.

Max Dupain: pages 231; 134.

The source of the quotations used in some of the monochrome captions is indicated by raised small capitals:

[A] Charles Darwin's Autobiography, edited by Nora Barlow, 1958.

[J] *Journal of researches into the Natural History and Geology of the countries visited during the voyage of HMS Beagle round the world,* by Charles Darwin, 1890.

[L] Charles Darwin's letters to his family, 1831–6. From *Charles Darwin and the voyage of the Beagle,* edited by Nora Barlow, 1945.

[N] Volume II of *Narrative of the surveying voyages of HMS Adventure and Beagle between the years* 1826 *and* 1836, by Robert FitzRoy, 1839.

[CD] *Charles Darwin's Autobiography, with notes and letters depicting the growth of the 'Origin of Species',* by Francis Darwin, 1961.

LIST OF ILLUSTRATIONS

COLOR

From *Zoology of the voyage of HMS Beagle.*

Page 149 Argentinian oppossum *(Didelphis crassicaudata)*. From *Zoology of the voyage of HMS Beagle.*

Page 150 A bromelia found in the Andes *(Bromelia bicolor)*. From *Historia fisica y politica de Chile,* by Claudio Gay, 1854.

Page 159 A family of Araucanian Indians. From *Historia fisica y politica de Chile.*

Pages 160-1 Costumes of the Chilean rustics. From *Historia fisica y politica de Chile.*

Page 162 A collection of coleoptera found in Chile. From *Historia fisica y politica de Chile.*

Page 171 The town of Talcahuano and port of Concepcion. From *Vues et paysages des régions équinoxiales.*

Page 171 Silver and copper works in the Andes. From *Travels into Chile.*

Page 172 Carrion-feeding hawk *(Caracara vulgaris)*. From *Historia fisica y politica de Chile.*

Page 197 The Galapagos turtle-dove *(Zenaida galapagoensis)*, by John Gould. From *Zoology of the voyage of HMS Beagle.*

Pages 198-9 *Midshipman's berth,* by Augustus Earle. *National Maritime Museum, Greenwich. Photo : Derrick Witty.*

Page 200 The cactus-feeding finches *(Cactornis scandens)*, by John Gould. From *Zoology of the voyage of HMS Beagle.*

Page 209 Species of the Doris, found in the southern Pacific. From *Voyage de la corvette l'Astrolabe . . . pendant les années 1826, 1827, 1828 et 1829,* by J. D. d'Urville, 1830-5.

Page 210 A Maori chief, wearing the feather-trimmed cape of his rank. From *New Zealanders illustrated,* by G. F. Angas, 1847.

Page 219 Monument to the daughter of a Maori chief. From *New Zealanders illustrated.*

Pages 220-1 *Tahiti, revisited,* by William Hodges. *National Maritime Museum, Greenwich.*

Page 222 Head of a New Zealander with tattooes. From *Voyage de l'Astrolabe.*

Page 231 *Papeete harbour, Tahiti.* Watercolour by Conrad Martens. Collection of Mrs T. H. Odillo Maher, Sydney.

Page 231 *Dawes Point, Sydney.* Watercolour by Conrad Martens. *By courtesy of the Mitchell Library, Sydney.*

Page 232 Head of an Australian aborigine. From *Voyage de découvertes aux terres australes,* by F. Péron, 1807-16.

Page 241 Entrance to Port-Jackson. From *Views in Australia or New South Wales,* by J. Lycett, 1824.

Page 241 Hobart Town, Tasmania. From *Views in Australia or New South Wales.*

Pages 242-3 *A Bible-reading on board ship,* by Augustus Earle. *National Maritime Museum, Greenwich.*

Page 244 The platypus *(Ornithorhynchus anatinus)*. From *Voyage de découvertes aux terres australes.*

Page 244 The King Island emu *(Dromiceius diemenianus)*. From *Voyage de découvertes aux terres australes.*

Page 253 Sea perches *(Plectropomidae)* from King George's Sound. From *Voyage de l'Astrolabe.*

Page 253 Baby Australian sea-lion *(Neophoca cinerea)*. From *Voyage de l'Astrolabe.*

Page 254 The wallaby, or short-tailed kangaroo *(Setonix brachyurus)*. From *Voyage de l'Astrolabe.*

MONOCHROME

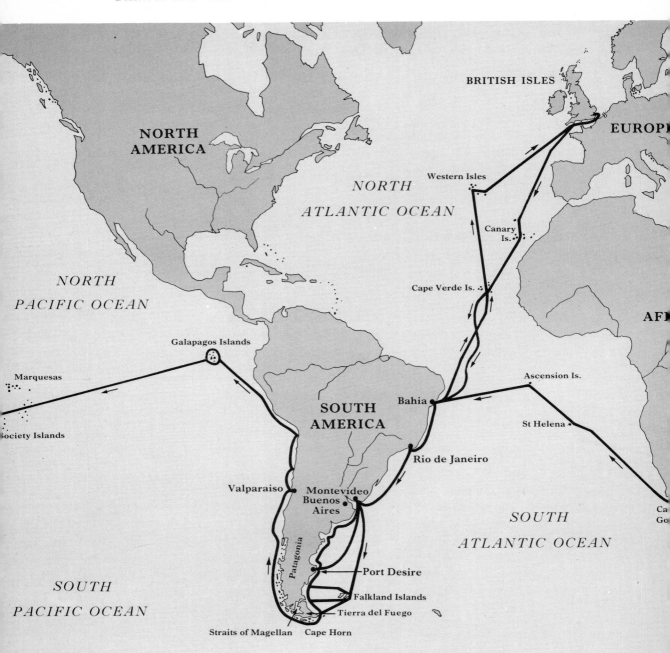

The voyage of the Beagle

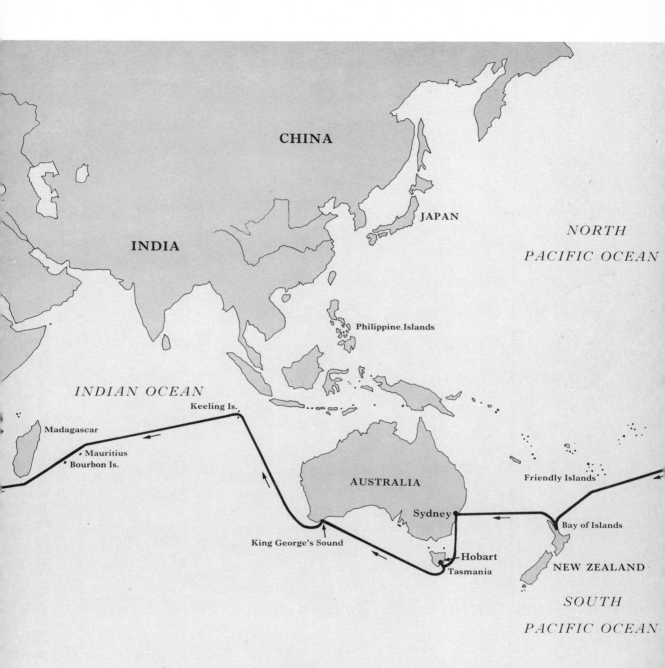

CHINA

INDIA

JAPAN

NORTH

PACIFIC OCEAN

Philippine Islands

INDIAN OCEAN

Keeling Is.

Madagascar

Mauritius
Bourbon Is.

AUSTRALIA

Friendly Islands

Sydney

Bay of Islands

King George's Sound

Hobart

Tasmania

NEW ZEALAND

SOUTH

PACIFIC OCEAN

17

Christ's College. 'During the three years which I spent at Cambridge, my time was wasted, as far as the academical studies were concerned, as completely as at Edinburgh and at school.' ^

CHAPTER I

THE MEETING

One of the fascinating things about Charles Darwin is that he really does seem to have been one of those men whose careers quite unexpectedly and fortuitously are decided for them by a single stroke of fortune. For twenty-one years nothing much happens, no exceptional abilities are revealed; then suddenly a chance is offered, things can go either this way or that, but luck steps in, or rather a chain of lucky events, and away he soars into the blue never to return. It all looks so inevitable, so predestined; yet the fact is that in 1831 no one in England, certainly not Darwin himself, had the slightest inkling of the extraordinary future that lay ahead of him, and it is next to impossible to recognise in the brooding, ailing figure of the later years this blithe young extrovert on the brink of his greatest adventure – the voyage of the *Beagle*.

Events moved so quickly that he could hardly take in what was happening. On 5 September 1831 he was summoned to London to meet Robert FitzRoy, captain of HMS *Beagle,* a ship which the Admiralty was sending off on a long voyage round the world, and the suggestion was that Darwin should be offered the post of naturalist on the voyage. It was an astonishing idea. He was only twenty-two years old, he had never met Captain FitzRoy, and a week ago he had never even heard of the *Beagle*. His youth, his inexperience, even his background, seemed all against him; yet against all these odds he and FitzRoy got on famously and the offer was made.

The *Beagle,* FitzRoy explained, was a small ship, but a good one. He knew her well; he had taken over the command on her previous voyage to South America, and had brought her back to England. Now she was being entirely refitted at Plymouth and she had a splendid crew, many of whom had sailed in her before and had volunteered for this new voyage. They had two missions: first they were to continue the charting of the South American coast, and secondly they were to get a more accurate fixing of longitude by carrying a chain of chronological reckonings round the world. The ship would set off in a matter of weeks; they would be away more than two years, perhaps even three or four, but Darwin would be free to leave the ship and return home whenever he chose to do so. He would have ample opportunities for getting ashore, and in the course of the voyage they would be doing many exciting things, exploring unknown rivers and mountains, calling at coral islands in the tropics and sailing far down towards the frozen south. Oh, it was all wonderful. 'There is indeed a tide in the affairs of men', Darwin wrote to his sister Susan, 'and I have experienced it'.

He was in fact remarkably fortunate. In the first place it was most unlikely that he and FitzRoy should have got on as well as they did; indeed, it would be hard to imagine two characters in England who by nature and training were more opposed. At almost every point they were in conflict. Whereas the Darwins were upper-class Whigs and Liberals, the FitzRoys were most decidedly aristocrats and Tories. Charles Darwin was the son of a country doctor – a very successful one, it must be said – and the grandson of another, Dr Erasmus Darwin, who had made a great name in the world both as a medical practitioner, at which he made a small fortune, and as a writer of verse with scientific and evolutionist themes. The FitzRoys were descended from the illicit liaison between Charles II and Barbara Villiers, the Duchess of Cleveland, and Robert FitzRoy himself, the son of Lord Charles FitzRoy, was a grandson of the Duke of Grafton and a nephew of Castlereagh.

He looked it. The head was proud and authoritarian, the expression disdainful, and although his figure was slight his whole bearing was that of a man accustomed to privilege. Unlike Darwin, he had had the very opposite of an easy, cosseted life; since the age of fourteen, when he entered the Royal Naval College, he had been recognised as a naval officer of exceptional ability. Even in an age when promotion was given very early to outstanding men, especially if they had high connections, it was remarkable that he should have taken over command of the *Beagle* in South America, when he was only twenty-three.

But FitzRoy enjoyed authority. His values were fixed. He knew precisely what was right and what was wrong, and without being by any means a stupid or uneducated man he was intolerant of all speculation and half shades of meaning. Already he was a deeply religious man, he

LEFT Robert FitzRoy in his late twenties. 'He was a handsome man, strikingly like a gentleman, with highly courteous manners . . .'ᴬ RIGHT Charles Darwin as a young man. After their interview, FitzRoy wrote to the Admiralty Hydrographer: 'I like what I see of him much, and I now request that you will apply for him to accompany me as naturalist.'

believed every word in the Bible absolutely, and these spiritual certainties were transferred to his practical life; upon his quarter-deck he was a martinet. The other expected qualities followed; he was brave, he was resourceful, he was efficient and he was just. But then there was another side to his character; inside this tight outward sheath there was a suppressed restlessness, a yearning for something that was missing – perhaps warmth and affection – and it broke through occasionally in acts of great generosity and contrition. There was no room for compromise in this nature, no slack to be taken up and let go again, no real patience, and so he vacillated between moods of depression and elation, and by the time this interview with Darwin took place he was already giving way to those manic-depressive tendencies that were to end in his suicide thirty-four years later.

FitzRoy was a little cool when they first met. He was an arrogant young man. He had heard that Darwin was a Whig and when Darwin walked into the room he took a dislike to him, particularly his nose; it was not the nose of a man who could endure the rigours of a voyage around the world. But Darwin's natural easy enthusiasm swept away all stiffness; before the interview was over FitzRoy was begging him not to be too hasty in giving a yes or no, and reassuring him about the terrors of the sea. FitzRoy seems to have realised that he was dealing with an exceptional young man. He was perhaps a little too naïf, a little too well cared-for, but definitely intelligent. Was he tough enough? – that was the question. Would he crack up when they got to sea?

Darwin on his side was charmed beyond all reason. Never had he met such a man before, such perfect manners, such quiet power and authority, such understanding, the very beau ideal of what a captain ought to be. One also gathers that Darwin sensed very clearly the doubts that were in FitzRoy's mind, the suggestion that the job would prove too much for him. A challenge was being offered. Well and good, he decided, he would accept it, he would show this splendid man just what he could do. He would not let him down.

Let us look back for a moment at Darwin's life as it had been up to the moment of this meeting, the meeting which was to decide the voyage that became, as it were, the origin of the Origin of the Species, and the basis of those ideas which have since changed all our lives. Let us forget that sad, shawl-covered old man who is the image of the Charles Darwin we know so well, and turn to him as he was in 1831 when he had just received his degree as Bachelor of Arts at Cambridge. An observer standing in the lovely court of Christ's College might well have seen him riding in from hunting, a slim, tall figure in a red coat, not really a handsome young man but one with very pleasant good looks; a well-set head with a broad brow, direct and friendly brown eyes, no beard as yet (though there were sideburns), and the fresh complexion of a twenty-two-year-old who spends a good deal of his time out of doors. A groom would have taken his horse in the court, and he would have gone running up a short stone staircase to the first floor, where he lived in a large, square, panelled room that was heated in winter by an open fireplace.

Christ's in those days had a reputation for 'horsiness', a thing that suited young Darwin very well, for he loved to hunt and to shoot, and

Charles Darwin in 1840. Watercolour by George Richmond.

in his room he used to practise his marksmanship by throwing up his gun in front of a mirror, or, if he was giving a party, by getting one of his companions to wave a candelabra of lighted candles about while he snuffed out the flames with a blank cartridge. (He once wrote to a friend: 'upon my soul, it is only about a fortnight to the "First", then if there is a bliss on earth that is it'.) There was a certain amount of drinking at these parties – he was a member of the Glutton Club – and they usually ended the evening with a little music and a game of *vingt-et-un*.

It was not then the room of a very diligent student; 'I'm through, through, through' he exclaimed with relief and surprise when he scraped through his examinations with a pass, and it was not thought remarkable that without being specially religious he was destined now to enter the Church as a country parson; lots of well-to-do young men did that. For the rich it was an urbane age. One would have noticed that he was popular with his companions. 'At breakfast, wine or supper parties', wrote a contemporary of his later, 'he was ever one of the most cheerful, the most popular and the most welcome'. And there were sometimes up to sixty guests at these parties. He was healthy, his manner was diffident but he was full of enthusiasms, and he had no doubts at all about the world he lived in; he enjoyed it and he did not want to change it.

Upon just one count he was unusual, and that was in his quite spontaneous and exceptional interest in natural history. Everything in the fields delighted him. Flowers, rocks, butterflies, birds and spiders – from boyhood he had collected them all with the sort of absorption that belongs only to the besotted amateur or the true professional. Just now his passion was beetles, and he had his cases of specimens laid out in his room. One day he saw two rare beetles on a piece of bark and seized them both, one in each hand; then he saw a third and new kind which he could not bear to lose, so in order to release his right hand he popped a beetle into his mouth. It instantly ejected an acrid and burning fluid which forced him to spit it out, but all he cared about was losing two valuable specimens. He even employed an assistant to collect for him, and when he discovered that the man was secretly giving the best specimens to a rival coleopterist he threatened to kick him down the stairs.

This passion for collecting, however, like hunting and shooting, he regarded as something on the side, as a hobby and entertainment; the true business of life was concerned with the classics, which he loathed,

Robert FitzRoy, after his promotion to Vice-Admiral, by Francis Lane.

with mathematics, which he could not understand ('I suppose you are two fathoms deep in mathematics', he writes to a friend who has not answered his letters, 'and if you are, then God help you, for so am I, only with this difference, I stick fast in the mud at the bottom and there I shall remain'), and with the Church, though he privately doubted if he had a true vocation for it. Yet Professor Henslow, who lectured to him at Cambridge, was a clergyman and also Professor of Botany, and Henslow had greatly encouraged him in his interest in natural history; he had invited him to his celebrated Friday evenings for discussion, he had taken him on botanising walks and boating excursions along the river Cam, and he had even persuaded Darwin to study geology, a subject which he had shied away from at first. During his last year at Cambridge Darwin was distinguished as 'the man who walks with Henslow'. There was no reason why he should not continue with his collecting and his sports when he settled into his vicarage in the country.

Even in his family background Darwin was fortunate. His grandfather, Dr Erasmus Darwin, had been a much respected if slightly controversial figure; he had worked on the idea of evolution, though he never brought it to a conclusion. Coleridge coined the word 'darwinising' to describe his rather wild theorising. Erasmus for his part described a fool as someone who 'has never made an experiment in his life'. He belonged to a scientific club in Birmingham called the Lunar Club, naturally nicknamed 'The Lunatics', which investigated anything new.

Charles's own father Robert had also gone in for medicine, and had done very well in practice at Shrewsbury, where he had built a fine house, The Mount, above the river Severn. Charles was a little frightened of his father. Robert was a huge man, six feet two in height, 328 lbs in weight, and rather autocratic in his ways; his family used to say that when he returned home in the evenings it was like the tide coming in. Yet his son also loved him. Many years later when Charles was an old man he told his daughter that he thought his father had been a little unjust to him when he was young, but had made up for it by his kindness later. The suggestions made recently that his feelings of inferiority towards his father may have affected his development, and that the ill-health of his later life was due to his anxiety and feelings of inadequacy as a child, do not seem very convincing. It was true that Charles's mother had died when he was eight, but his three older sisters had been devoted to him

ABOVE LEFT Christ's College, from the court. RIGHT John Stevens Henslow. 'He was free from every tinge of vanity or other petty feeling; and I never saw a man who thought so little about himself or his own concerns. His temper was imperturbably good, with the most winning and courteous manners.' A   BELOW The English bridge at Shrewsbury.

LEFT Dr Erasmus Darwin, Charles Darwin's grandfather. Frontispiece of *The Botanic Garden*. RIGHT Dr Robert Darwin. 'He was a man of a quick, vivid temperament, with a lively interest in even the smallest details in the lives of those with whom he came in contact.' CD

and had brought him up, and he was evidently a tough little boy for he always remembered awaiting some reproof from his sister Caroline and making himself 'dogged' so as not to care what she might say. At eight years old he was already taking a passionate interest in gardening and the different sorts of animals he saw round the countryside, and many years later he wrote of the pleasure he had had at the age of ten and a half 'on a blowy day walking along the beach by myself and seeing the gulls and cormorants wending their way home in a wild and irregular course'.

Then there were his cousins, the Wedgwoods, the famous family of potters, who lived in a grand house, Maer Hall, only twenty miles away.

Susannah Wedgwood, later Charles Darwin's mother, with her brother Josiah (centre) and their family. Their father was the founder of the Wedgwood potteries.

Charles was forever riding over there, and he was a great favourite of his Uncle Jos and Aunt Bessie and their four daughters, especially Emma. It was a world of well-staffed country houses, of coaches and grooms, of partridge shooting in the autumn and hunting in the winter, of dinner parties and elegant clothes, of the comfortable knowledge that he would come into a very adequate fortune later on.

School, certainly, had not been much of a success; he had always been below average and Julian Huxley is probably right when he says that with today's standards he would never have got into a modern university. At the local school in Shrewsbury they had tried without success to drum classics into him, and then he had gone on to study medicine at Edinburgh, which was a failure; among other things he could not stand the sight of blood. Later he came to regret bitterly that for this reason he had never studied dissection seriously. He did, however, attend Jameson's lectures on geology, and though he found them dull it was through him that he became acquainted with the Curator of the Museum who was a great enthusiast in Natural History. Darwin read a paper before the Plinian Society on microscopic marine animals, and learned to stuff birds and animals from a negro who had travelled with Waterton.

But all that was behind him now; his father had let him abandon medicine and go on to Cambridge, and if he had frittered away his time at Cambridge and had learned very little there, at least he had enjoyed it; at least now in 1831 he had his degree in his pocket and the pleasant prospect of the summer vacation before him. 'During midsummer geologised a little in Shropshire', he wrote in his diary.

Then he went for a trip through Wales with another of his new-found scientific friends, Adam Sedgwick, the Professor of Geology at Cambridge. They seem to have spent some pleasant weeks studying rock formations and working on a geological map of the country, and it was not until 29 August that Darwin returned to his home in Shrewsbury. He then learned from his father and sisters that a letter (which they appear to have read) had arrived from Professor Henslow. Enclosed with it was another letter from George Peacock, a Cambridge mathematician and astronomer who was responsible for nominating naturalists to naval ships making surveys; in it he made that completely unexpected offer to young Darwin of the post of unpaid naturalist aboard HMS *Beagle*. Here was a bolt from the blue. He had never thought of himself as a serious naturalist, a professional naturalist, or indeed eligible for any scientific job; he was to be a clergyman. Then again this bizarre proposition cut so drastically across his plans; after the partridge shooting he had hoped to make a journey down to the Canary Islands before taking holy orders. And yet – why not? He was inclined to accept. Henslow, who had recommended him to Peacock, was most pressing that he should. Henslow himself had nearly taken the job, Darwin told his sister Susan, but 'Mrs. Henslow looked so miserable that Henslow at once settled the point'.

Dr Darwin had other views. He thought it was a wild scheme; Charles had already switched from medicine and now he was running away from the Church; he was not used to the sea and would be away for two years or more; he would be uncomfortable; he would never settle down after he got back; he would harm his reputation as a serious clergyman; others must have been offered the post before him, and since they had refused there must be something fishy about it; in short, a useless undertaking.

Dr Darwin did not absolutely forbid Charles to accept the appointment, but he made himself emphatic. 'If', he said, 'you can find any man of common sense who advises you to go I will give my consent'.

Charles was in no position to argue. His allowance (which he had overspent at Cambridge) was his only source of income, and although subconsciously he may have wanted to get away from his father he would never have dreamed of defying his authority. Reluctantly he wrote to Henslow saying that he could not go.

At least it was something that the partridge season was about to open, and on the following day he rode over to the Wedgwoods' house to be ready for the opening shoot. Unlike his brother-in-law, Dr Darwin, Josiah Wedgwood was a supple and humorous man. His house, Maer, was a light-hearted place, overflowing with guests, and always something amusing was happening there – very unlike The Mount, where Dr Darwin's overwhelming presence forced a certain gravity on his family. Uncle Jos was young Darwin's means of escape from his father; he had made journeys with him to Scotland, to Ireland and to France, he had confided in him, and now he told him about the offer of the *Beagle* post and of his refusal.

Wedgwood did not at all agree with Dr Darwin. He thought it was a splendid opportunity and that it ought not to be turned down. He got Darwin to write out the list of Dr Darwin's objections, and he had an answer to every one of them. Kindled by this Darwin decided to tackle his father again. He wrote him a hesitant letter: 'My dear Father – I am afraid I am going to make you again very uncomfortable . . . The danger appears to me and all the Wedgwoods not great. The expense cannot be serious, and the time I do not think, anyhow, would be more thrown away than if I stayed at home. But pray do not consider that I am so bent on going that I would for one *single* moment hesitate, if you thought that after a short period you should continue uncomfortable . . .'

This done and the letter sent off, he turned to the pleasant prospects of the morrow. He was out with his gun and his dog soon after breakfast and family prayers on the following morning, and it was barely ten o'clock when a servant came to him with a message from his uncle saying that the *Beagle* offer was too important to be left in abeyance; they must drive over to The Mount together and get his father to change his mind. There may have been an ulterior motive behind Wedgwood's persistence. We do not quite know how strongly Charles at this stage was attracted by his daughter Emma. Certainly the liking was there, certainly in that household of young girls they must have thought that Charles might want to marry one of them one day. It seems possible therefore that Josiah might well have said to himself that this young fellow ought to have a little more experience of the world, ought to prove himself, before he would be eligible as a suitor.

LEFT Adam Sedgwick, Professor of Geology at Cambridge. Darwin once described him as a 'talking giant'. RIGHT Letter from Charles Darwin to his father, 31 August 1831, begging him to reconsider his refusal to let his son join the *Beagle* expedition.

At all events, from this point onward – the turning-point of Darwin's life* – events accelerate. On arrival at The Mount Uncle Jos took the doctor's objections one by one and demolished them. Charles, feeling guilty about his extravagance at Cambridge, dropped in a word about money: 'I would have to be deuced clever to spend much money aboard ship', to which his father replied, 'they say you *are* very clever'. But in the end the doctor was won round, and Charles, in a great state of excitement, dashed off a letter cancelling his earlier refusal; he would be 'very happy to have the honour of accepting'. He was now in a fever of anxiety that he was too late, that the job had already been offered to someone else, and at 3 a.m. on the following morning, 2 September, we find him aboard the express coach, the *Wonder*, en route to Cambridge. He arrived very tired at the Red Lion Hotel late that night, and sent a note round to Henslow asking if he could meet him first thing in the morning.

Henslow had bad news for him; a Mr Chester, a naturalist of some standing, was also being considered for the post. All would depend on what sort of impression Darwin made upon FitzRoy, the captain of the *Beagle*, since FitzRoy had made it clear that he would only take a man whom he personally liked – a not unreasonable condition since he was going to share his cabin with the naturalist throughout the voyage. On 5 September Darwin set off for London. He managed to get an appointment with FitzRoy that same day, and, as we have seen, the interview went splendidly.

The two men met again next day and things went just as well. FitzRoy had been quite exceptionally frank and kind, Darwin wrote to his family. He had said: 'Now your friends will tell you a sea captain is the greatest brute on the face of creation; I do not know how to help you in this case, except by hoping you will give me a trial'. Their quarters on board would be cramped, and the captain had been very honest about it: 'He asked me at once, "Shall you bear being told that I want the cabin to myself, when I want to be alone. If we trust each other this way, I hope we shall suit; if not probably we should wish each other at the Devil" '.

The expenses would not be great; his mess bills would amount to only £30 a year, and a round sum of £500 ought to see him through the whole voyage. Would Susan get the servants at The Mount busy over

---

*Charles was well aware of the importance of his uncle's decisive action. Three years later he wrote to his sister Catherine: 'I have not forgotten the comfort I received that day at Maer, when my mind was like a swinging pendulum'.

The coronation of William IV and Queen Adelaide, 8 September 1831. Darwin spent a guinea for a seat and wrote to his sisters that it was 'like only what one sees in picture-books of Eastern processions'.

his kit? 'Tell Nancy to make me soon 12 instead of 8 shirts; tell Edward to send me up in my carpet-bag (he can slip the key in the bag tied to some string) my slippers, a pair of lightish walking-shoes – my Spanish books, my new microscope (about six inches long and 3 or four deep) which must have cotton stuffed inside; my geological compass, my Father knows [where to find] that; a little book, if I have got it in my bedroom – *Taxidermy*'. Then there were firearms he must have – FitzRoy said that at many places it would not be safe to go ashore without a brace of pistols – but these he could get in London.

The city was bedecked with flags and gas illuminations, crowns and anchors and 'WRs', for the coronation of William IV, and since the shops were shut on 6 September Darwin bought a seat to watch the procession go by and joined the crowds watching the fireworks that night. Next day he was off in a gig round the town with FitzRoy, his shopping list in his hand. The city was so crowded the carriages could barely crawl along Regent Street. FitzRoy, it turned out, was a mighty spender, he thought nothing of giving £400 for his personal firearms, and Darwin was sufficiently carried away by this extravagance to part with £50 for a 'case of good strong pistols and an excellent rifle'. There was so little time; they would sail in October. 'I feel my blood run cold at the quantity I have to do.' And he went on again about FitzRoy: '. . . he is everything that is delightful. If I was to praise him half so much as I feel inclined, you would say it was absurd . . .'

On 11 September the two of them set off to see the *Beagle* in the dock-yards at Plymouth.

LEFT Microscope used by Darwin during the voyage. RIGHT Darwin's pistols. 'He [FitzRoy] recommends me strongly to get a case of pistols like his, which cost £60! and never to go on shore anywhere without loaded ones . . .'[L]

35

Plymouth dockyard, *c.* 1815. Detail from a painting by Nicholas Pocock.

CHAPTER II

THE DEPARTURE

They took three days to sail around from London, three days of talking and exploring one another's personality, and Darwin's admiration for FitzRoy steadily increased. 'Perhaps', he wrote to Susan, 'you thought I admired my beau ideal of a captain in my former letters: all that is quite a joke to what I now feel. Everybody praises him (whether or no they know my connection with him), and indeed, judging from the little I have seen of him, he well deserves it. Not that I suppose that it is likely that such violent admiration as I feel for him can possibly last; no man is a hero to his valet, as the old saying goes; and I certainly shall be in much the same predicament as one'.

FitzRoy on his side was equally if less exuberantly impressed; in letters he wrote later on he goes out of his way to praise young Darwin; he was just the man he wanted. It was nothing unusual to take a naturalist on board a voyage such as this, but FitzRoy had also a special object in view, a religious object, and it is more than likely that he took this opportunity – the trip to Plymouth – to explain the matter.

The voyage, he believed, would provide a grand opportunity to substantiate the Bible, especially the book of Genesis. As a naturalist, Darwin might easily find many evidences of the Flood and the first appearance of all created things upon the earth. He could perform a valuable service by interpreting his scientific discoveries in the light of the Bible. Darwin, the young clergyman-to-be, was very ready to agree. He too, did not in the least doubt the literal truth of every word in the Bible at this time – it was part of the world he accepted and liked so well – and if he could be of use in this way, well then, that made the prospect of the voyage all the more exciting. Of course other influences had already been at work upon him. It is reasonable to suppose that as Erasmus's grandson he had read some of his work, notably the famous poem *Zoönomia,* although he later denied that he had been influenced by it in any way. At Cambridge he had read Fleming's *Philosophy of Zoology,* Burchell's *Travels,* Scrope on volcanoes, Caldcleugh's *Travels in South America,* and he probably knew something of Lamarck's and Buffon's early theories of evolutionary change. We know that he had read von Humboldt, the German naturalist, with such enthusiasm that he had planned a journey to Madeira months before the idea of the *Beagle* arose, and that Humboldt's *Personal Narrative* was one of the few books he took with him.

It seems quite certain, however, that at this point Darwin had not yet even begun to dream of the work he was to accomplish. He was barely more than a schoolboy, full of adolescent enthusiasm. He began to wish, he wrote to Susan, that they would be away longer and travel further than had been planned. Writing to FitzRoy about the sailing date he said: 'My second life will then commence, and it shall be as a birthday for the rest of my life'.

But then everything pleased Darwin through these days. The *Beagle,* then lying dismasted in dry-dock, was indeed very small, a ten-gun brig of 242 tons, only 90 feet in length, into which seventy-four people would have to stow themselves. But 'no vessel', he wrote, 'has been fitted out so expensively and with so much care. Everything that can be is made of mahogany'. (Actually she had been found to be so rotten after her last voyage that she was practically being re-built.) The officers, compared to the captain, were rather small fry, but they were evidently a 'very intelligent, active, determined set of young fellows', though rather rough. There were John Wickham, the first lieutenant, James Sulivan, the second, John Lort Stokes, who would assist FitzRoy with the surveying, Robert MacCormick, the surgeon, and his assistant Benjamin Bynoe, George Rowlett, the purser, Midshipman King and an artist, Augustus Earle – all of them at this stage merely anonymous faces to Darwin, but soon in that small ship to become very definite individuals. The rest of the crew was made up of the master and his two mates, the boatswain, the carpenter, clerks, eight marines, thirty-four seamen and six boys. Finally there were three passengers, York Minster, Jemmy Button and a young girl, Fuegia Basket. These were three natives from Tierra del Fuego, the icy territory about Cape Horn. FitzRoy had picked them up on the previous voyage, had bestowed their whimsical names upon them (Jemmy had been bought for a few buttons), and for a year had had them

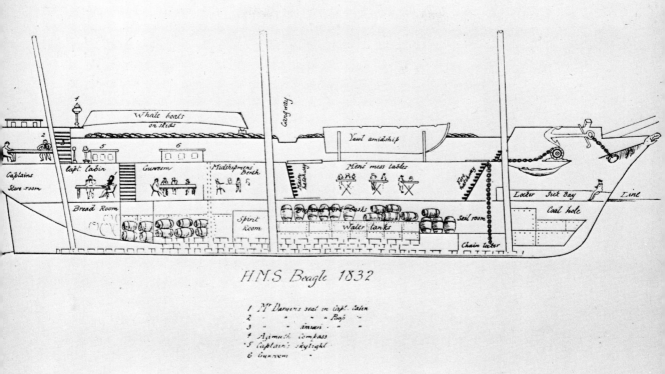

Side-elevation of the *Beagle*. After he first saw the ship, Darwin wrote to Henslow: 'The absolute want of room is an evil that nothing can surmount'.

educated at his own expense in England. He had showed them off to King William and Queen Adelaide; the Queen put one of her bonnets on Fuegia's head and a ring on her finger, and gave her a purse of money to buy clothes. Now, with a smattering of English, their European clothes and a stock of European goods and chattels, they were to be returned to their homes on the other side of the world to spread Christianity and civilisation among their countrymen. A young missionary, Richard Matthews, had volunteered to go with them.

There was a round of farewells with Charles coaching up to London and Cambridge and back to Shrewsbury to make his final arrangements. Books – he must have Humboldt, Milton and the Bible, Lyell's first volume on *Principles of Geology* (a parting gift from Henslow) just off the press; and the last additions to his equipment – binoculars, a geological

Catwater, Plymouth, from the citadel. 'These two months spent at Plymouth were the most miserable which I ever spent.'[A]

magnifying glass and jars of spirit for preserving specimens. On 24 October 1831 he arrived back at Plymouth only to find that the *Beagle* was not ready; a party including the Fuegians had come down by steam-vessel and 'not a few boats' were needed to transfer their baggage on board – wineglasses, butter dishes, tea-trays, soup tureens, a mahogany dressing-case, beaver hats and so on. But the repairs to the *Beagle* were taking much longer than had been expected.

The next two months for Darwin were perfectly miserable. He had nothing definite to do. 'My chief employment', he wrote to his family, 'is to go on board the *Beagle* and try to look as much like a sailor as ever I can. I have no evidence of having taken in man, woman or child'. The combination of the winter weather, homesickness, and the reaction from his first excitement about the voyage filled him with misgivings and made him ill. A rash broke out on his hands and painful palpitations in his chest made him think he had heart disease. But he dared not go to a doctor lest he be told that he could not sail. He took rooms ashore and spent part of his days stowing and re-stowing his kit in his tiny cabin – and indeed there was very little room; FitzRoy, with his passion for exactness, had set up no less than twenty-two chronometers packed in beds of sawdust on shelves, and Darwin's sleeping space was so confined that he had to remove a drawer from a locker so as to accommodate his feet.

FitzRoy himself continued to be very kind. There was just one odd little incident. They went into a shop in Plymouth one day to exchange a piece of crockery which had been bought for the ship. When the dealer refused to make the exchange FitzRoy flew into a rage. To punish the man he enquired the price of a very expensive set of china, and then said, 'I should have purchased this if you had not been so disobliging'. Then he stalked out of the shop. Darwin well knew that FitzRoy never had any intention of making such a purchase – they had all the crockery they wanted – but he said nothing and they walked along in silence. Then suddenly the captain's anger evaporated: 'You didn't believe what I said?' 'No', Darwin replied, 'I did not'. FitzRoy said nothing for a few minutes and then burst out: 'You are right. I acted wrongly in my anger at the blackguard'.

By December the *Beagle* was ready, but her first attempts to get to sea were an ominous warning of what lay ahead. On 10 December and again

41

on 21 December the vessel set out, only to be driven back into Plymouth again, and on each occasion Darwin was violently seasick. On Christmas Day the crew got drunk in port, and Midshipman King, the duty officer, was forced to put one sailor in chains for insolence. It must have been an uproarious spree since the men were not sufficiently recovered to man the sails on the following day. 27 December broke cloudy and calm, but during the morning the wind freshened from the right quarter, the east; one could see the smoke streaming away from Plymouth's chimney pots. FitzRoy and Darwin lunched ashore on mutton chops and champagne, and came on board at 2 p.m. Now at last they were away, the men keeping time to the coxswain's pipe as they pulled away at the cables, and by dusk that night Darwin was forlornly watching the Eddystone Lighthouse drop below the horizon – his last view of England. They headed through heavy seas across the Bay of Biscay and out into the grey Atlantic. FitzRoy had the worst of the Christmas rioters brought out on deck and flogged.

These early weeks were clouded over and made a blank in Darwin's mind by his illness. 'The misery I endured from sea-sickness', he wrote sadly home, 'is far beyond what I ever guessed at . . . The real misery only begins when you are so exhausted that a little exertion makes a feeling of faintness come on – I found nothing but lying in my hammock did any good'. He could eat nothing but raisins. Occasionally he dragged himself out on deck for a breath of fresh air, but the racing waves and the heaving deck were too much for him; most of the time he simply lay in his hammock or perched himself on FitzRoy's sofa, trying to read. By night he shared the poop cabin with Midshipman King, and being right in the stern it must have heaved about a good deal in bad weather. He was too ill even to get up and see the coast of the island of Madeira as they sailed by, and at snow-capped Teneriffe there was a bitter disappointment when no one could go ashore because of the quarantine regulations; they feared cholera from England.

There was an additional agony for Darwin in all this; the thought that FitzRoy was finding him too soft for the voyage. For the moment there was nothing to be done about it; he could only complain as little as possible, set his teeth, and hold on, hoping for better days. Whatever happened he was not going to throw in his hand and go home as soon as they made a landfall; upon this point he was absolutely set. And in the end he was rewarded. At the Cape Verde islands there was a respite when

Santa Cruz de Teneriffe, a bitter disappointment to Darwin when he found he could not go on shore.

they were at anchor for twenty-three days while FitzRoy fixed the exact position of the islands, and here for the first time Darwin got an inkling of what this voyage might mean to him. This was the first time he had seen a volcanic island; he had been deeply absorbed in Lyell's book, and the thought now passed through his mind that *he* might one day write a book on geology. Fifty years later he could remember the exact spot where the idea came to him. 'That was a memorable hour for me, and how distinctly I can call to mind the low cliff of lava beneath which

43

I rested, with the sun glaring hot, a few strange desert plants growing near, and with living corals in the tidal pools at my feet.'

Already Darwin was noting, collecting, recording, observing. Not a single item was allowed to get past his scrutiny: birds, the landscape, the natives, the dust, the plants. He observed in detail a sea-slug, the *Aplysia,* dissected it and found in its stomach several small pebbles. In his notes there is a drawing of a baobab tree, but this was probably done by FitzRoy; Darwin could not draw. He wrote to Henslow that only one thing worried him – whether he was noting the right facts, the important facts; 'in the one thing collecting, I cannot go wrong'.

After the Cape Verde islands they paused briefly at St Paul's Rocks, a small archipelago about 600 miles off the coast of Brazil. They were astonished at the vast numbers of birds which covered the rocks and rose

Porto Praya, Cape Verde Islands. 'The neighbourhood of Porto Praya, viewed from the sea, wears a desolate aspect. The volcanic fires of a past age, and the scorching heat of a tropical sun, have in most places rendered the soil unfit for vegetation.' ¹

in great circling flocks almost blacking out the sky. A boat-load of sailors at once set off joyfully for the shore, and fell on the birds like schoolboys, knocking them out with the ends of their rifles or with their bare hands. The unfortunate birds were of two species, boobies and terns, and even Darwin observed that 'both are of a tame and stupid disposition and are so unaccustomed to visitors that I could have killed any number of them with my geological hammer'. The sailors returned to the *Beagle* with a great heap of fresh meat, to find another boat's crew had started fishing and were pulling up enormous groupers as fast as they let their lines down. A shoal of sharks appeared and rushed at the groupers as the lines were being pulled in; the sharks were quite fearless and seized the fish even while the men were beating the sea with their oars.

Then they went on again across the equator, meeting blessedly calmer water as they approached Brazil. Dolphins sported round the ship and seabirds followed steadily on behind. Darwin began to come to life again. He was a conspicuous figure on board; while the crew were in naval uniform he continued in the civilian clothes of a gentleman of the early nineteenth century – the top-coat with its tails, the double-breasted waistcoat with its lapels and many buttons, the long trousers, the high-collared shirt with its cravat. Moreover, his activities seemed to the crew very strange; he made himself a 4 foot tow-net of bunting, and by trailing it out astern was able to haul up myriads of tiny coloured sea creatures that oozed and glistened on the deck.

The day's routine was simple and spartan. Breakfast was at eight, and FitzRoy and Darwin ate alone in the captain's cabin. Directly the meal was over – and neither of them waited until the other was finished – they went off to their work: FitzRoy to make his morning round of the decks, and Darwin, if the weather was calm, to deal with his marine animals, dissecting, classifying and making notes. If it was rough he went back to bed and tried to read. Dinner at 1 p.m. was a vegetarian meal, rice, peas and bread and water. No wine or liquor was ever served. At 5 p.m. they had supper, which might include meat and such anti-scorbutic things as pickles, dried apples and lemon juice. In the evening there was much slow talk, with the officers hanging over the rails under the tropical sky. 'I find a ship a very comfortable house', he wrote to his father, 'with everything you want, and if it was not for sea-sickness the whole world would be sailors.' And then again to his sister Caroline: 'One part of

45

Crossing the equator on board the *Beagle*. 'This most disagreeable operation consists in having your face rubbed with paint and tar, which forms a lather for a saw which represents the razor, and then being half drowned in a sail filled with sea-water.' [L] Drawing by Augustus Earle.

my life as sailor . . . is unexpectedly pleasant; it is liking the bare living on blue water'.

As the days went by Darwin found himself drifting into a strange ambivalence in his relations with FitzRoy. He had been much touched when he had first come on board by FitzRoy himself showing him how to sling his hammock and stow his things, and the captain continued to show him every kindness. (It was during this period that FitzRoy wrote back to England: 'Darwin is a very sensible hard-working man, and a very pleasant mess-mate. I never saw a "shore-going fellow" come into the ways of a ship so soon and so thoroughly as Darwin'.)

But FitzRoy was such a contradictory sort of man, so nervous, so touchy. Darwin was not becoming disillusioned about him, he was still a great man, but there was a side to his nature that was something less than beau ideal. There had been the incident in the crockery shop back at Plymouth, and then the flogging of the Christmas day roisterers; Darwin had not thought it fair that the men should be allowed to drink if they were to be punished for it afterwards. But he had not dared to protest. It had not taken him long to realise that the captain of a naval vessel was a law unto himself. He could not be spoken to or argued with as an ordinary man, and at the same time FitzRoy drove himself unnecessarily hard. 'If he does not kill himself, he will during the voyage do a wonderful quantity of work', Darwin wrote home. '. . . never before have I come across a man whom I could fancy being a Napoleon or a Nelson. *I should not call him clever;* yet I feel nothing is too great or too high for him. *His ascendancy over everybody is quite curious . . . Altogether he is the strongest marked character I ever fell in with'.*

FitzRoy's precarious temper was worst in the morning when he made his round of the ship, and if the slightest thing was amiss he would come down on the offender with evangelical wrath, almost as though he had suffered a personal insult. His appearance on deck was electrifying; a group of sailors hauling on a rope would fling themselves into the work as though their lives depended on it. Junior officers coming on duty had a way of enquiring: 'Has much hot coffee been spilled this morning?', meaning: 'How is the Captain's temper?' But it was FitzRoy's 'severe silences' that Darwin found hardest to bear; morose, gloomy and threatening, he would sometimes abandon himself to his black moods for hours at a stretch. All this did not make FitzRoy hated; everyone admired his

47

wonderful seamanship, he had his sunny days, and generally his manners were courteous and charming. Still, one watched one's step aboard the *Beagle,* and Darwin had to learn the arts of turning away wrath.

With the rest of his shipmates Darwin got on very well. Everyone liked him. He was shy, and he was eager to learn. To the crew he was known affectionately as 'our flycatcher'. The second lieutenant Sulivan, who afterwards became Admiral Sir James Sulivan, wrote later: 'I can confidently express my belief that during the 5 years in the *Beagle* he [Darwin] was never known to be out of temper, or to say one unkind or hasty word to anyone . . . this, combined with the admiration of his energy and ability, led to our giving him the name of "the dear old Philosopher" '. Wickham, the first lieutenant, railed against the mess made by Darwin's specimens on the decks, but he was gay and friendly, 'by far the most conversible being on board', and Bynoe, the assistant surgeon, had become a special friend. Young Philip King, the midshipman, was a spirited boy: 'I have read all Byron', he declared, 'and I don't care a damn for anyone'.

Augustus Earle, the artist, was an exceptional man. He was the son of an American painter who had settled in England, and had himself studied at the Royal Academy in London, where he had proved to be adept at almost any kind of painting, portraiture, landscape, or historical. His other passion was wandering round the earth in places where no other artist had ever been. When he joined the *Beagle* at the age of thirty-seven (which made him almost the oldest man in the ship), he had already been travelling for thirteen years and had lived in both South America and Australia, two of the principal areas for which the *Beagle* was bound. Like Darwin, he was an enthusiast for Humboldt, especially his descriptions of the tropical forest. They got on so well together that they decided they would share a house ashore when they got to Brazil.

Then there were the Fuegians. York Minster was a taciturn and moody character, but it was obvious that he was growing very fond of Fuegia Basket, and she of him. Jemmy Button, a boy of sixteen, was everyone's favourite. Darwin seems to have liked them all, and as the only university man on board he probably took a hand at little Fuegia Basket's education. But he was particularly attached to Jemmy. The boy was rather a dandy in his white kid gloves and highly polished boots. Accustomed all his life to the sea he simply could not understand Darwin's illness. He would

The Fuegians in 1833, drawn by FitzRoy. ABOVE LEFT Jemmy Button: 'he used always to wear gloves, his hair was neatly cut, and he was distressed if his well-polished shoes were dirtied'. ABOVE RIGHT Fuegia Basket: 'a nice, modest, reserved young girl, with a rather pleasing but sometimes sullen expression'. BELOW York Minster: 'his disposition was reserved, taciturn, morose, and, when excited, violently passionate'.[1]

gaze down on him in his misery, murmuring, 'Poor, poor fellow'. And as he turned away he tried not to smile. The Fuegians had remarkably acute eyesight, much sharper than the sailors', and when Jemmy quarrelled with the officer on watch he would say, 'Me see ship, me no tell'.

As a landsman and a novice at sea Darwin naturally had his leg pulled from time to time. 'A Grampus Bear to port', Sulivan shouted down to him in his cabin one day. Darwin rushed on deck to be met with a shout of laughter. It was 1 April. However, he scored a point in his favour when he managed to hook a large shark on a line trailed over the stern.

The ship made good time, averaging around 160 miles every twenty-four hours. Sixty-three days out from England they reached San Salvador, and landed at the beautiful ancient town of Bahia, set in a wild luxuriant greenness of oranges, bananas and coconuts. Darwin's first experience

San Salvador, Bahia, overlooking the Bay of All Saints. Drawing by Augustus Earle.

of a tropical forest was ecstatic. 'Delight', he wrote in his journal, 'is a weak term to express the feelings of a naturalist who for the first time has wandered by himself in a Brazilian forest . . . such a day brings a deeper pleasure than he can ever hope to experience again'. He was, he felt, like a blind man who has just been given eyes, looking at a scene 'like a view in the Arabian Nights'. Then again: 'A most paradoxical mixture of sound and silence pervades the shady parts of the wood. The noise from the insects is so loud that it may be heard even in a vessel anchored several hundred yards from the shore; yet within the recesses of the forest a universal silence appears to reign'.

On 18 March 1832 they continued southwards down the Brazilian coast. On the night of 3 April they were becalmed outside Rio de Janeiro, but on the following morning they were able to sail into the beautiful

Mole, palace and cathedral at Rio de Janeiro. Drawing by Augustus Earle.

harbour in bright sunshine. The city was a very much smaller place than it is now – suburbs like Botofogo were open countryside – but there was a great deal of activity in the harbour. A squadron of British men-of-war was at anchor there, and on the mole long lines of half-naked negro slaves were carrying cargo down to the trading ships. In the background the palace and the cathedral rose out of the maze of narrow streets, where priests in cone-shaped hats and Spanish ladies in carriages were going by, and the peak of Corcovado soared up into the clear blue sky. Elated with the prospect of getting off the ship and beginning his botanising and collecting, Darwin hurried ashore and took up quarters in the town. Now at last he could start to prove his usefulness as a scientist – perhaps even with luck do something to please FitzRoy by relating his discoveries to the great religious truths of the Bible.

A view of the coast of Brazil.

CHAPTER III

THE TROPICAL FOREST

Within three days Darwin had arranged to join an Irishman named Patrick Lennon who was about to visit his coffee plantation 100 miles away to the north. They were a party of seven, all mounted on horseback. In hot sultry weather they followed the coast for the first few days, and then turned inland into the tropical rain forest. To say that Darwin was happy is not enough, he was enthralled, enraptured. All round them vast ceiba trees and cabbage palms, as slender and tall as ships' masts, rose up and with their foliage blotted out the sun. From the topmost branches Spanish moss and long rope-like lianas trailed down through the green light, and in the silence and stillness of the midday heat the great blue morpho butterfly came sailing by. The air was filled with the scent of aromatic plants – camphor and pepper, cinnamon and clove. Then there were the monstrous anthills, twelve foot high, the parasitic orchids sprouting from the tree trunks and the incredibly brilliant birds: the toucans and the green parrots, the tiny humming-bird with its invisibly fluttering wings poised above a flower. Darwin made quick ecstatic jottings in his notebooks as he rode along: 'Twiners entwining twiners – tresses like hair – beautiful lepidoptera – silence – hosannah'.

The blood-curdling cry of the howler monkey erupted through the silence and this was followed by a distant roar like heavy surf falling on a beach – the approach of a storm. Great warm raindrops broke through the canopy of leaves above their heads and in a moment they were drenched. Fresh earthy smells came up into the washed air from the ground, and all the valleys about them were filled with billowing lakes of white mist. Then as the storm passed and it grew dark a tremendous commotion began: the nightly concert of the frogs, the cicadas and the crickets, and the flickering of the fireflies in the darkness. 'Every evening after dark this great concert commenced; and often have I sat listening to it, until my attention was drawn away by some curious passing insect.'

The Toco toucan (*Ramphastos toco*), by John Gould.

ABOVE 'The contrast of the palm-trees growing amidst the common branching kinds, never fails to give the scene an inter-tropical character.'ᴶ BELOW LEFT A giant ants' nest. Some were nearly twelve feet high. RIGHT The anaconda, or aquatic boa, another giant product of the tropical forest, can reach a length of thirty feet.

Yet there was a terrifying ferocity in this abundance. One day he got down from his horse to watch a fight to the death between a *Pepsis* wasp and a large spider of the genus *Lycosa*. The wasp made a sudden dart from the air, thrust home its sting and then flew off. Though badly wounded, the spider was just able to crawl into a tuft of grass and hide, and for some time the wasp ranged back and forth unable to find it. When at last, by an involuntary movement, the spider gave itself away, the wasp came in for the kill with wonderful precision – two quick stings on the underside of the thorax. Then the victor alighted and began to drag the body away. Darwin did the irrational thing that most of us would have done; he drove the wasp away from its victim.

Further on they came upon one of the most devastating sights in the forest – a march of the army ants. As the shining, black, many-headed horde came on – it was a hundred yards long – every living thing in its path was thrown into panic. It was marvellous to see how the lizards, the cockroaches and the spiders, driven mad by fear, were cut off by a fast encircling movement and then in an instant the ravening mass fell upon its prey.

So then amid all this beauty there was a never-ending menace. Nothing was safe. To prey and to be preyed upon, that was the condition of existence, and the weak in order to survive had to camouflage themselves. Into Darwin's collecting jar went the phasmid stick, the insect that resembled a twig of dry wood, the harmless moth that disguised itself to look like a scorpion, the beetle that put on the colours of poisonous fruit to save itself from the birds. He noted that the horns of certain species are mere ornament, worn for sexual attraction, but most features were intended to deceive: some moths, for instance, had windowed wings to imitate dead leaves with holes; others like the cosmid moth looked like fallen flowers; others again had glaring luminous false eyes. Some insects protected themselves by impersonation; the Distasteful heliconian is unpalatable to predators, so other species, themselves edible, wore the heliconian's warning colours.

How Henslow would have enjoyed all this. 'I never experienced such intense delight', Darwin wrote to him ecstatically. 'I formerly admired Humboldt, I now almost adore him; he alone gives any notion of the feelings which are raised in the mind on entering the Tropics . . . I am at present red-hot with Spiders . . . and if I am not mistaken I have already

OVERLEAF 'Forests and flowers and birds I saw in great perfection, and the pleasure of beholding them is infinite.' L

'The trees were very lofty, and remarkable, compared with those of Europe, from the whiteness of their trunks.' [J]

taken some new genera . . . I shall have a large box to send very soon to Cambridge.'

At this point he got his first attack of fever, and felt so ill that he thought he would fall off his horse, but 'cinnamon and port wine cured me in a wonderful manner'.

And now abruptly Darwin was made aware that the brutality in nature, the persecution of the weak by the strong, applied to human beings as well. They had entered a part of the forest where the track had become overgrown, and a negro slave with a sword had been sent ahead to cut a way through. Darwin was trying to speak to this man in broken Spanish, and was gesticulating to emphasize his meaning when he observed with a sense of shock that the man thought he was about to be struck. He cringed, dropped his hands, and held up his face, waiting submissively for the blow to fall. Darwin was horrified. Were all the slaves as terrified as this, so broken in spirit? Lennon, who was a considerable slave-owner, no doubt reassured him. But could one be reassured? Presently they rode up to a bare, steep-sided granite hill where for a time a group of runaway slaves had managed to hide themselves and to scratch a living from the soil. They had even built themselves a little group of grass huts which were a replica of the homes that they had once known before they were captured in Africa. The huts were now deserted. A party of Brazilian soldiers had ambushed the place and had captured all the runaways with the exception of just one woman, who had preferred death to the prospect of being enslaved again; she had thrown herself off the summit of the hill and had been dashed to pieces on the rocks below. 'I was told before leaving England', wrote Darwin to his sister Caroline, 'that after living in slave countries all my opinions would be altered; the only alteration I am aware of is forming a much higher estimate of the negro character'.

As they approached Lennon's hacienda a cannon was fired and a bell began tolling to announce their arrival – a strong eruption of sound in the deep silence of the forest – and the plantation slaves came out to meet them. It was a delightful place, a quadrangle of thatched huts with the master's quarters on one side and on the other sides the stables, the plantation storehouses and the sleeping quarters of the slaves. In the house the gilded chairs and sofas which could have come from any Victorian drawing-room looked oddly out of place with the whitewashed walls, the thatched roof and the windows with no glass. Stacks of coffee beans were piled up in the centre of the yard, and there was a great come and go of chickens and dogs, of horses and farm animals, of women gathered round their cooking fires and naked children playing in the sun.

A gargantuan meal was prepared for the guest – Darwin had hardly finished the turkey when he was confronted with roast pig – and all the while the pulsating life of the plantation kept moving around them. Children, chickens and dogs – 'sundry old hounds' – strayed in through the open sides of the hut and had to be chased away by a slave who was specially kept for that purpose.

Lennon, the absolute ruler of this little feudalistic world, was something of an enigma in all this. During the ride up from Rio de Janeiro he had seemed to Darwin to be a reasonable and fair-minded man, but now suddenly, for no apparent reason at all, he flew into a violent rage with the manager of the place, a man named Cowper. Perhaps it was the heat, perhaps it was the persistence of the intruding children, perhaps it was a long-standing grievance between them, but at all events Lennon was beside himself with fury. He announced that he was going to sell off all his female slaves and their children; they were to be separated from their husbands and fathers and marched off to Rio to be sold at public auction. In particular he proposed to get rid of a mulatto child of whom the manager was very fond. It was at this stage that both men drew their pistols and might have opened fire had not Darwin and the others intervened.

The quarrel was forgotten by the morning. But the fact that the sale could have taken place, that Lennon could have broken up these families who had been living together for many years, and that few people would have thought that there was anything cruel or inhuman about it – all this to Darwin was a shocking and a monstrous thing. Nor was he reassured when in the morning the whole community gathered in the quadrangle for prayers and the singing of hymns. The negro voices rose with great sweetness in the morning air, and Lennon blessed them all before they set out for work.

Darwin had been brought up with a detestation of slavery – in England the Wedgwoods were among the earliest campaigners against it – and he was still brooding on what he had seen, and the cruelty and the hypocrisy with which it was overlaid, when he got back to Rio de Janeiro. Here

ABOVE Negro huts in a plantation. BELOW LEFT Female slaves and their children. RIGHT Wedgwood cameo, used as anti-slavery propaganda in Erasmus Darwin's time.

Slave-drivers punishing negroes. 'It makes one's blood boil, yet heart tremble, to think that we Englishmen and our American descendants, with their boastful cry of liberty, have been and are so guilty . . .'¹

his indignation was brought to the boil again by the discovery that the old lady who lived opposite him kept screws to crush the fingers of her female slaves, and in the house where he was staying a young mulatto was 'reviled, beaten and persecuted enough to break the spirit of the lowest animal'.

'I thank God', he wrote later, 'I shall never again visit a slave country. To this day, if I hear a distant scream, it recalls with painful vividness my feeling when, passing a house near Pernambuco, I heard the most pitiable moans, and could not but suspect that some poor slave was being tortured, yet knew that I was as powerless as a child to remonstrate . . .

Rio family going to mass. 'I never saw any of the diminutive Portuguese, with their murderous countenances, without almost wishing for Brazil to follow the example of Hayti.' ᴸ

I have seen a little boy, six or seven years old, thrice struck with a horse-whip (before I could interfere) on his naked head, for having handed me a glass of water not quite clean; I saw his father tremble at a mere glance from his master's eye'.

It made one's 'blood boil but heart tremble' to think that Englishmen and Americans were also involved in the slave traffic. He talked about it to FitzRoy when they were on board the *Beagle* one day. FitzRoy's views about slavery were what one might have expected; without actually condoning it he thought there was a good deal to be said in its favour. The system was a very old one, as old indeed as the Bible, and it should

65

Corcovado mountain, Rio de Janeiro, at the foot of which Darwin and Augustus Earle shared a cottage. Drawing by Augustus Earle.

not be tampered with too readily, especially by liberal-minded idealists who had never had to undertake the responsibility of running an estate. Now, when Darwin began to recount his adventures, he listened calmly enough at first. He said that he too had made a visit to one of the plantations while Darwin was away, and had found the slaves living in conditions that were every bit as good as those of the agricultural labourers in England. The owner of the plantation had called up a great many of his men, and he personally had asked them if they were unhappy and wished to be free. All had answered 'no'.

Darwin was too angry to be prudent. What other possible answer, he demanded, could they have given in their master's presence? His tone of voice and his contemptuous smile infuriated FitzRoy. If Darwin doubted his word, he burst out, then he had better get out of the cabin; it was impossible for them to live together any longer. Darwin thought that he would do better than that; he would get off the ship as well. And with that he walked out.

No one was disposed to take sides with FitzRoy in this affair. Directly they heard of the quarrel the other officers came to Darwin and said that he would be very welcome to move his belongings in with them. Meanwhile FitzRoy had sent for Wickham and was working off his rage by pouring forth a tirade against Darwin and everything he stood for. But little by little he calmed down, and, as it always happened with that tense, wrought-up nature, remorse set in. He had gone too far. He had been wrong. He had hurt Darwin's feelings. He must get him back.

Presently Wickham emerged on deck; the captain wished to present his apologies to Mr Darwin and requested him to come back to his cabin. Darwin was very ready to accept. After all, it was the great adventure of the voyage that mattered; by now it had gathered a rhythm of its own and it was more important than any private quarrel.

Perhaps it was fortunate that in any case they were to be parted for the next few months; while FitzRoy went north again with the *Beagle* to continue his survey of the coast, Darwin lived ashore at Rio with Augustus Earle and Midshipman King. Darwin enjoyed himself immensely. 'You cannot imagine anything more calmly and delightfully than these weeks have passed by', he wrote, this time to his other sister Catherine. 'There never was a greater piece of good luck than the *Beagle* returning to Bahia.' They shared a very pleasant cottage at Botofogo at the foot of Corcovado

OVERLEAF Different species of Brazilian trees and shrubs. Darwin thought that the most remarkable thing in the tropics was the novelty of vegetable forms.

V.

VI.

VII.

IV.

III.

Gez. v. Helmuth v. Kiesewetter.

VIII.

IX.

X.

(his board and lodging only cost 22s. a week, he was relieved to find), and he was soon engrossed in collecting specimens – spiders, butterflies, birds and seashells – and packing them up to send to Henslow.

One can get some idea of the meticulous labour involved in this packing from the letter which Henslow wrote to Darwin when he received the box in Cambridge some six months later. 'I think you have done wonders', he wrote, but he urged him to use more paper, and not so much tow. One excellent crab had lost all its legs, a bird had its tail feathers crumpled, two mice were rather mouldy. The tiny insects were most excellent, but perhaps it was dangerous to their antennae and legs to pack them in cotton. It must have been very tantalising for Darwin to have to wait so long for news of his precious boxes. In one instance the letter of acknowledgment itself took seven months to reach him, making it a year or more since the package had been sent off.

While Darwin collected, Earle painted the tropical scenery, and no doubt helped him in making drawings of some of his specimens. He made one hunting expedition with an old Portuguese priest, but only succeeded in getting a few small green parrots and toucans; his companion, however, shot two large bearded monkeys. 'These animals have prehensile tails, the extremity of which, even after death, can support the whole weight of the body. One of them thus remained fast to a branch, and it was necessary to cut down a large tree to procure it.' Darwin would not easily let any specimen go. 'I am becoming quite devoted to Natural History; you cannot imagine what a fine miserlike pleasure I enjoy when examining an animal differing widely from any known genus.'

His experiments were esoteric: he made frogs walk up panes of glass, he fed glow-worms raw meat, he observed in great detail the springing power of a luminous beetle, and he found a butterfly which ran along the ground. On one day alone, 23 June, he caught sixty-eight species of a particularly minute beetle.

When the *Beagle* got back it brought the calamitous news that a party had gone up the river from Rio snipe-shooting, all had got fever, and three of them had died; one of these was Charles Musters, the son of a friend of FitzRoy's and a great favourite on board. Everybody's spirits were low, and they were now all eager to get away on the next stage of the voyage, though Darwin was not so keen on the long days at sea. 'How glad I am that the *Beagle* does not carry a year's provisions; formerly

70   The black trogon *(Trogon viridis)*, by John Gould. OVERLEAF LEFT The Eurynome Hermit, a species of humming bird *(Phäethornis eurynome)*, by John Gould. RIGHT The purple-stained Laelia orchid *(Laelia purpurata)*, by L. Constans.

PLATE 96.

L. Constans del. & pinx.

Printed by C.J. Greffing, Leiden.

Pl. 15

FELIS Geoffroyi.

it was like going into the grave for that time.' But already he referred to the *Beagle* as home; he took great pride in her and continually spoke of her beating other ships at manoeuvres. 'I find they all say we are now the no. 1 in South America', he wrote home with some pleasure. 'It is a great satisfaction to know that we are in such beautiful order and discipline.'

Now they were off on the cruise down to the far south of the continent, the virtually unknown lands of Patagonia and Tierra del Fuego. 'I long', Darwin wrote, 'to set foot where no man has trod before'.

On a bright day early in July the *Beagle* stood out to sea. She was given an unexpected and rousing send-off by the other British men-of-war in port; as the little ship sailed out sailors manned the rigging of the huge *Warspite,* three cheers sounded across the water, and a band struck up with the song *To Glory you Steer.*

Monkey and its young.

Reconstruction of the skeleton of a *Megatherium*.

CHAPTER IV

THE ANTEDILUVIAN ANIMALS

Darwin was seasick again as soon as they reached the open ocean. On many days he hung about the deck forlornly or retreated to his hammock. There is a rather sad little entry in his notebook for 16 July 1832: 'Much sea-sick. Flying fish – porpoises'. He was not one of those who grow used to the sea, and at the end of the voyage he was just as bad a sailor as when he first left Plymouth. As late as March 1835 he was writing home: 'I continue to suffer so much from sea-sickness that nothing, not even geology itself, can make up for the misery and vexation of spirit'. But unless it was physically impossible he was never idle while at sea. He was up and out with his telescope whenever there was anything to see; he spent long days watching and thinking about the vast numbers of birds that he saw, and came to the conclusion that the instinct for migration takes precedence over all others. 'Everyone knows how strong the maternal instinct is; nevertheless, the migratory instinct is so powerful that late in autumn some birds desert their tender young, leaving them to perish miserably in their nests.' He remarked on a goose he had been told of which, when its wings were clipped, migrated on foot.

Whales broke the surface and spouted alongside the ship, and once when they were travelling at nine knots under full canvas hundreds of dolphins appeared. For a long time they sported back and forth around the *Beagle,* criss-crossing in front of the bows and leaping clear out of the sea. Then, as the ship continued south, they saw barking or jackass penguins, a species that yaps like a dog. One night when they were anchored in the estuary of the Rio Plata, St Elmo's fire lit up the mastheads and the rigging, and the penguins, darting through the water, left long trails of phosphorescence in their wake. 'Everything is in flames', Darwin wrote to Henslow, 'the sky with lightning, the water with luminous particles, and even the very masts are pointed with a blue flame'.

In Rio de Janeiro Robert MacCormick, the surgeon, had left the ship.

Dolphin belonging to a new species which Darwin named after FitzRoy *(Delphinus fitzroyi)*. The gesture was returned when FitzRoy called a mountain in Tierra del Fuego after his companion.

He seems to have been generally disliked, and even Darwin remarked 'He's no loss'. The man who took his place, however, young Benjamin Bynoe, was a very agreeable fellow, and by now had become a good friend of Darwin's. He shared Darwin's enthusiasm for natural history, he made excursions ashore with him whenever he could, and he did what he could for Darwin's sea-sickness. Bynoe had been on the previous voyage, and was able to supply many useful tips; he was also a man with whom Darwin could let off steam after his brushes with FitzRoy. One of the nice things about Bynoe was that he took great care of the Fuegians and Jemmy Button was devoted to him.

They were travelling now out of the tropics into the cool temperate zone, and in fresher, bluer seas the men put on heavier clothes. Darwin, along with the officers, began to grow a beard and looked, he says, 'like a half-washed chimney-sweeper'. On Sunday mornings FitzRoy conducted divine service, and it must have been a fine sight to see him standing there on the afterdeck with the men gathered before him and the sails billowing overhead. Little Fuegia Basket and her two companions would be got up in their Sunday best, and all around them were the things that had grown so familiar they hardly saw them any more; the muskets, the pistols and the cutlasses clamped to the wall behind the wheel, the wheel itself with 'England Expects Every Man To Do His Duty' engraved on the rim, and on the hub a drawing by Augustus Earle of Neptune and his trident; and the never-ending sea beyond. FitzRoy, with his passionate fundamentalism, can hardly have failed sometimes to have read the lesson from the Book of Genesis: 'And God made the beast of the earth after his kind, and cattle after their kind, and every thing that creepeth upon the earth after his kind; and God saw that it was good.

'And God said, Let us make man in our image, after our likeness; and let them have dominion over the fish of the sea, and over the fowl of the air, and over the cattle, and over all the earth . . .'

One almost hears that clear authoritarian voice explaining: 'But this man whom God had created became corrupt and filled the earth with violence. And so God flooded the earth for a hundred and fifty days and destroyed him. Yet in His great mercy God allowed Noah to build an Ark and take on board it his family and two each, a male and a female, of every living creature, and all these were saved. Thus the world as God created it in the beginning has been preserved to this present day. Let all of us then in this ship remember this divine providence and humbly ask for His blessing on our voyage into the uncharted seas that lie ahead . . .' The scene is evoked by Earle's painting *Divine Service on Board a British Frigate*, which he later exhibited at the Royal Academy in London.

FitzRoy was always at his best at sea. Here, in the narrow space of his ship, the complications and untidiness of life ashore were put away, things could be properly controlled and organised; a high polish on the brass cannon and the right set of the sails. The struggle against the sea was a clean and decent issue, nothing to be afraid of. Whatever else they thought of their captain aboard the *Beagle* no one ever doubted his courage: 'I would sooner go with the Captain with 10 men than with anybody else with 20', Darwin wrote home to his sister Susan. 'He is so very prudent and watchful as long as possible, and so resolutely brave when pushed to it.'

And so they were all exhilarated when they ran into trouble in the

Rio Plata. A twenty-eight-day cruise down from Rio had brought them up to the roadsteads of Buenos Aires, and they were about to sail into port when the Argentinian guardship opened fire upon them. The first shot was a blank, the second was live and sent a splutter of bullets whistling over the *Beagle's* rigging. FitzRoy sailed on to his anchorage, and at once dispatched two boats to the shore with a demand for an explanation. Before the men could land a customs officer came out and ordered them back on board again, saying that they must submit to a quarantine inspection. By now FitzRoy was in no mood to submit to anything. He ordered the ship to put about, ran out his guns and then sailed down close to the guardship. He hailed her as they went by and said that if she dared to fire another shot he would send his whole broadside into her rotten hulk. With that he ran down the muddy tide of the Plata to Montevideo, where the British frigate *Druid* was at anchor. It was soon arranged that the *Druid,* with her guns ready, should sail at once for Buenos Aires to demand an apology from the Governor. As with everybody else, Darwin's blood was up. 'Oh I hope the guardship will fire a gun at the Frigate. If she does it will be her last day above water.'

Meanwhile it looked for a moment as if he would get all the action he wanted nearer at hand; a government minister came out to the *Beagle* in a great state with the news that the black troops in Montevideo had risen in rebellion; would FitzRoy send a force ashore, if only to protect the property of the British merchants there? Yes, FitzRoy replied, he certainly would. He himself went ahead to reconnoitre and directly he reached the mole sent a signal for the *Beagle's* men to come ashore. Fifty-two of them, armed with muskets and cutlasses, got out the boats, and presently they were all marching up the main street – Darwin with his two pistols in his belt and a sword in hand – to take possession of the central fort. But alas, nothing happened, the rebels melted away, and after a night spent cooking beefsteaks in the fort the *Beagle's* assault force tamely returned to the ship.

A day or two later the *Druid* got back with a handsome apology from Buenos Aires, and the news that the captain of the guardship had been arrested. It had hardly been a famous victory; still, they had shown the Argentinians what was what, it had bound the *Beagle's* company much closer to her captain, and they were all in good spirits as they sailed on down the barren coast to the south.

Mole and customs house at Montevideo. Drawing by Augustus Earle.

About this time Darwin had acquired an assistant named Sims Covington, who had formerly been listed on the *Beagle*'s books as 'Fiddler and Boy to the Poop Cabin'. Darwin had taught him how to skin and stuff birds and other creatures, and to help in the general work of collecting, and as time went by he let him do more and more of the practical work, even finally, a year or two later, giving him his precious gun and doing no more himself of the shooting he had once so passionately enjoyed. Covington does not sound a very sympathetic character: 'My servant is an odd sort of person', wrote Darwin. 'I do not very much like him; but he is perhaps from his very oddity very well adapted to all my purposes.' The two seem to have got on well enough in the end, since Covington remained in Darwin's service for several years after the *Beagle* returned to England.

On 7 September they arrived at the little garrison township of Bahia Blanca, some 400 miles south of Buenos Aires, and here FitzRoy began his survey of the unmapped coastline of Patagonia. It was a desolate place. The wide, shallow bay was choked with mudbanks, and these

81

were covered with dreary reeds and swarming with armies of crabs. Inland no trees grew – it hardly ever rained – and a bleak wind swept across the flat plains of the Pampas. The Argentinian garrison consisted of a little group of ragged gauchos got up as soldiers, and they perched themselves in a fort that was surrounded by a ditch and a wall. Wild Indians (as distinct from those who had been 'tamed') were roaming about in the interior, and it was not safe for anyone to stray far away from the settlement. The soldiers were suspicious of the *Beagle* at first – she might be smuggling arms to the tribes or perhaps spying for a foreign power – and in particular they did not like the looks of *El Naturalista,* Don Carlos Darwin. What was a naturalist? What was he doing coming ashore with his two pistols stuck in his belt and his geological hammer in his hand? They followed him along the beach and watched with distrust when he began to hack away at some old bones embedded in a cliff.

Punta Alta, the scene of some of Darwin's greatest discoveries, both on this first visit and a year later, was a low bank on the shore some twenty feet in height, composed of shingle and gravel with a strata of muddy reddish clay running through it. The fossilised bones were found in the gravel at the foot of this cliff and were scattered over an area of about 200 yards square. At first Darwin could not make out what it was he was unearthing; there was a tusk, a pair of huge claws, a hippopotamus-like skull, a great scaly carapace turned to stone. One thing these relics shared in common, apart from their strangeness; they were all immense, all much bigger than the bones of any similar animal alive today.

Up to this time – 1832 – very little research had been made into the palaeontology of South America. Half a century before the skeleton of a *Megatherium,* a giant sloth, had been found in the Argentine and sent to Madrid, and von Humboldt and a few other travellers had unearthed some mastodon teeth, but little else was known, so it is easy to understand Darwin's excitement as these huge prehistoric forms began to take shape. 'The great size of the bones of the Megatheroid animals', he wrote in his journal, 'is truly wonderful'.

He and Covington set to work with pick-axes at Punta Alta. Time was short and Darwin became engrossed in his searches. 'Staid the night at Punta Alta in order for 24 hours of bone searching. Very successful with the bones, passed the night pleasantly.' More and more fossilised skeletons came to light, and were stacked upon the beach, and Darwin began to realise that he was dealing here with creatures that were virtually unknown to modern zoology, and which had vanished from the earth many milleniums ago. There were parts of that giant sloth, the monster that had once reached up its claws to feed on the tree-tops, and two other beasts, equally large and closely related, the *Megalonyx* and the *Scelidotherium* (he got a nearly perfect skeleton of this last one). Then there were the *Toxodon,* an animal like a hippopotamus and 'one of the strangest animals ever discovered'; the giant armadillo; the tusk of a *Mylodon,* an extinct elephant; a *Macrauchenia,* 'remarkable quadruped', and a guanaco (or wild lama) as big as a camel. All these bones were embedded in a thick matrix of seashells, 'a perfect catacomb for monsters of extinct races'.

For Darwin the important thing about these creatures was that, being different species, they nevertheless closely resembled their much smaller counterparts alive in the world today; the tiny sloths that lived in the trees, the little burrowing armadillo, the delicate guanaco. 'This wonderful relationship in the same continent between the dead and the living will, I do not doubt, hereafter throw more light on the appearance of organic beings on earth and their disappearance from it.' Where had these great beasts been at the time of the Flood? Perhaps most mysterious of all was the discovery of the bones of a horse. When the Spanish con-quistadors arrived in the sixteenth century the horse was unknown in South America. Yet here was definite proof that the animals had existed in the remote past. Did all this mean that the various species were con-stantly changing and developing, and that those which failed to adjust themselves to their environment died out? If this were so, then the present inhabitants of the world were very different to those that God had originally created; indeed, there could even be some doubt whether the Creation could have taken place within a single week; creation was a continuous process and it had been going on for a long time.

One problem that puzzled Darwin was that of the relation between the vegetation of the country and the number of animals; he finally made up his mind that quantity of vegetation was not essential, and as for the quality 'the ancient rhinoceros might have roamed over the steppes of central Siberia even in their present condition'. There was no evidence at all, he said, to support the idea that luxuriant tropical vegetation was necessary to these animals.

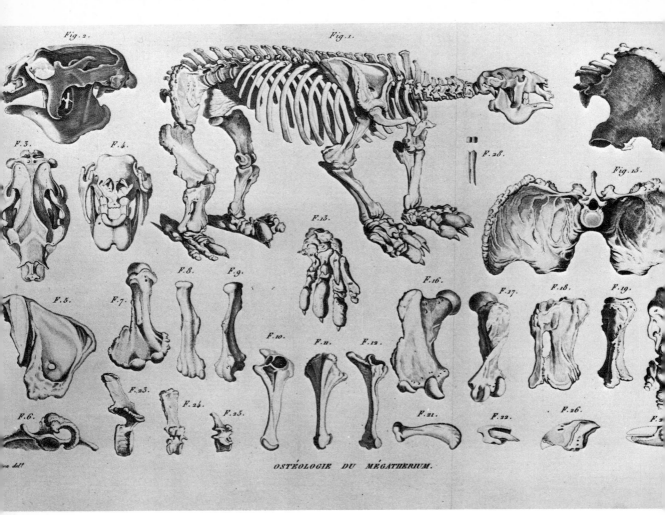

OSTÉOLOGIE DU MÉGATHERIUM.

Skeleton and bones of a *Megatherium*. 'As the only specimens in Europe are at Madrid . . . this alone is enough to repay some wearisome minutes.' ᴸ

Punta Alta was not the only site of Darwin's discoveries. On his later trip to Santa Fé he came across two immense skeletons projecting from the perpendicular cliff of the Parana river, but they were so decayed that he merely took away small fragments of the teeth. At Montevideo he heard of more fossil remains and went off to investigate them. These included the complete head of a *Toxodon,* and Darwin wrote sadly to Richard Owen, the naturalist, on the difficulties of fossil work: 'The head had been kept for a short time in the neighbouring farm-house as

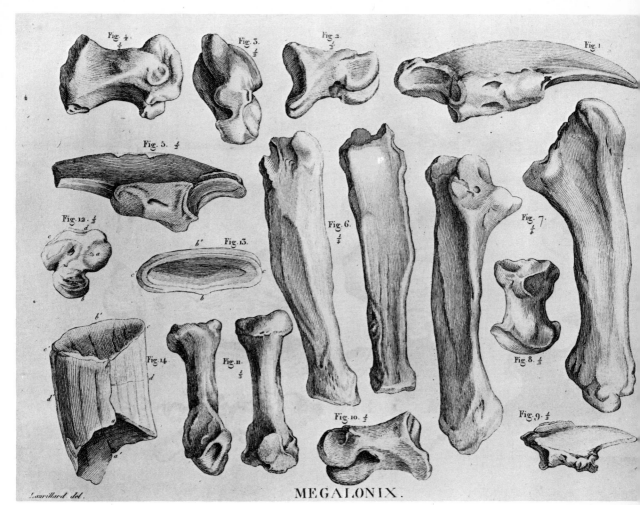

Bones of the *Megalonyx*.

a curiosity, but when I arrived it was lying in the yard. I bought it for the value of eighteen pence.' Apparently it had been quite perfect when found, but boys had been throwing stones at it and knocked out the teeth. In January 1834, at St Julian, Darwin found the skeleton of a *Macrauchenia* and wrote, 'we may conclude that the whole area of the Pampas is one wide sepulchre of these extinct quadrupeds . . .'. But 'the crust of the earth must not be looked at as a well-filled museum, but as a poor collection made at hazard'.

85

What then had exterminated so many species? 'Certainly no fact in the long history of the world is so startling as the wide and repeated extermination of its inhabitants.' He ruled out the possibility that changes in climate might have caused this extermination, and after considering many theories came to the conclusion that the isthmus of Panama might once have been submerged. He was right. For seventy million years there was no isthmus of Panama, South America was an island, and these great animals evolved in isolation. When the isthmus arose and North America was joined to South America the fate of these curious and largely helpless beasts was sealed.

When Darwin took his specimens back on board the *Beagle* Wickham was disgusted at the 'bedevilment' of his clean decks and railed against 'the damned stuff'. FitzRoy later on recalled 'our smiles at the apparent rubbish he frequently brought on board'. But to Darwin this was no light matter, and it must have been about this time that he first began to argue with FitzRoy about the authenticity of the story of the Flood. How had such enormous creatures got aboard the Ark? FitzRoy had an answer. Not *all* the animals had managed to get aboard the Ark, he explained; for some divine reason these had been left outside and drowned. But, Darwin protested, *were* they drowned? There was much evidence – the seashells, for example – to prove that the coast here had risen above the sea, and that these animals had roamed across the Pampas in much the same way as the guanacos did at the present time. The land had *not* risen, FitzRoy contended; it was the sea that had risen and the bones of these drowned animals were an additional proof of the Flood.

At this early stage of the voyage Darwin was not prepared to put his arguments too forcibly; he was puzzled, he needed more evidence, more time for thought. He was even willing to be persuaded that these new and disturbing ideas that were stirring in his mind were wrong. Certainly he had no wish to deny the truth of the Bible: 'No one can stand in these solitudes [the great forests] unmoved', he had written, 'and not feel there is more in man than the mere breath of his body.' It was just a matter of interpreting its words in the light of modern science. Here FitzRoy was very ready to help. One can see the two of them in the tiny cabin, the lamp swinging above their heads, the twenty-two chronometers ticking away, and the books spread out before them: FitzRoy's well-thumbed Bible, Lyell's second volume on Geology, which had just reached Darwin at Montevideo. Somehow, between them, they felt they would get at the truth.

The spring had arrived, and these were the pleasantest of days. Almost every morning Darwin was out with his new rifle getting fresh provisions for the ship. It was wonderful hunting; on some days he would bag as many as two or even three deer, and then there were the ostriches (not to speak of their huge and delicious eggs), the wild pigs (he shot one weighing 98 lbs), the armadillos, and the guanacos. The guanaco was a beast with an insatiable curiosity; Darwin found that if he lay on his back and kicked his legs in the air it would inevitably approach. Then he would jump up and take an easy shot. Ostrich dumplings and roast armadillo was a favourite meal on board, the one tasting like beef and the other like duck. FitzRoy bought a live puma from the Argentinian soldiers, and they skinned and ate that too. As for fish, they had all they wanted by dragging a net in the bay. Great shoals were hauled aboard and many unknown species appeared; Augustus Earle drew them and Darwin pickled them in spirits.

At the end of November 1832, well-fed, and all things going well on board, they made another trip to the Rio Plata and then turned south once more to carry out the experiment on which FitzRoy had set his heart: the landing of Jemmy Button and his friends in their homes in Tierra del Fuego and the setting up of a new outpost of Christianity on that remote and lonely coast. In the Bay of Good Success Darwin decided once and for all to dedicate his life to Natural History; he hoped to 'add a little to it'.

Reconstruction of the *Mylodon darwini*.

Detail from a painting by J. W. Carmichael, at one time thought to be of the *Adventure* and *Beagle* in the straits of Magellan.

CHAPTER V

TIERRA DEL FUEGO

The Fuegians on the whole had done very well on their year's voyage out from England. They had learned to speak English fairly fluently, they had absorbed – or appeared to have absorbed – FitzRoy's religious teachings, and they seemed to know what was expected of them. York Minster had announced that on getting ashore in his native territory he intended to marry Fuegia Basket. Latterly he had grown very jealous about her, as indeed he perhaps had need to be, since she was the only woman in the ship. He stood close by if any of the sailors talked to her and became sullen and morose whenever he was parted from her. Fuegia, if we are to trust FitzRoy's drawing of her (he was quite an efficient sketcher), had a pretty little face, and among the native Fuegians, who were hardly conspicuous for their good looks, might even have passed as a beauty. At Rio she had lived ashore for several months in the charge of an Englishman who had continued her instruction in the niceties of civilised living. Jemmy Button was as cheerful as ever and was eagerly looking forward to returning home. Even Matthews, the missionary, seemed to be facing up calmly and resolutely to his lonely and devoted exile.

All this was very good. Yet what a bizarre undertaking it was, how typical, when one comes to think of it, of FitzRoy. He alone on his own initiative had picked up these waifs three years before, and had tamed them in England, much in the same way as a man might catch a wild animal and domesticate it. And now, with no other guide than an inexperienced young missionary who had never been abroad before, he was about to turn them loose, not in some settled community, but in an unexplored region of howling gales and impossible cold where a few nomadic tribes scratched out a living that was as primitive as anything in the neolithic age. There was a rather touching arrogance about all this. Such was FitzRoy's faith that he really did believe that poor little

Fuegia Basket and her companions would be able to impart the divine light to the wild denizens of Tierra del Fuego. He had a theory that there were no such things as separate races of men in the world; we were all descended from Adam and Eve, who of course had sprung into existence fully grown and fully civilised – how else would they have kept themselves alive? But Adam and Eve's descendants had deteriorated; the further they had drifted away from the Holy Land to the more primitive parts of the world the more they had lost touch with civilisation. Hence these poor Fuegians. But they could be saved. All you had to do was to restore to them the civilisation and the knowledge of God which their first ancestors had had in the Garden of Eden.

It was one more touch of complete unreality in these proceedings that they had been supplied by the London Missionary Society with a stock of goods which might have been useful in an English village but were hardly likely to be of much help in this icy wilderness. Among other more sensible items they had been supplied with chamber-pots, tea-trays and crockery, wineglasses and soup tureens, beaver hats and white linen, and heaven knew what else in the way of dainty objects which were to reveal to the tribesmen how the great march of civilisation had gone on the other side of the world.

Tierra del Fuego has an appalling climate, one of the worst in the world. Even though she arrived there in midsummer the *Beagle* had to battle for a month against mountainous seas as she tried to round the Horn. Once a great wave engulfed her, carrying away one of the boats, and the little ship would have foundered had they not opened the ports and let the sea gush out in the nick of time. FitzRoy, being a great sailor, held on, and at last got them into a safe anchorage in Goree Roads at the entrance to the channel which had been named after the *Beagle* during her previous voyage. Glaciers reached down to the sea, and inland vast mountains covered with forests of beech and perpetual snow vanished into the swirling mists of a storm.

Darwin's first thought on catching sight of the native Fuegians was that they were much closer to wild animals than to civilised human beings (and this was a matter that was to strike him forcibly later on when he came to think and write about the descent of man.) They were huge creatures, with long matted hair and dark cadaverous faces which they painted in stripes of red and black, with white circles round their eyes.

Pampa Indians at a store in the Indian market of Buenos Aires.

They shaved their eyebrows and beards with sharp shells. Except for a short mantle of guanaco skin thrown over their shoulders they went naked. The colour of their skin was copper, and they coated themselves with grease. It was marvellous the way they could stand the cold. One woman who was suckling a baby came out to the *Beagle* in a canoe, and she sat there calmly in the tossing waves while the sleet fell and thawed on her naked breast. On shore these people slept on the wet ground while the rain poured through the roofs of their crude skin huts. They cultivated nothing; their diet was a mixed and moveable feast of fish, shellfish, birds, seals, dolphins, penguins, fungus and the occasional otter. Their language seemed to be made up of a series of guttural coughs. Yet they were not unfriendly and were not afraid. When Darwin went ashore with the sailors they clustered round him, patting his face and his body with great curiosity, and they were extraordinarily good mimics; every gesture he made and every word he uttered was perfectly imitated. When he made faces at them they grinned and made faces back at him, and they were delighted when the sailors began to sing and dance the hornpipe; delighted too when their tallest men were put back to back with the Englishmen so as to judge their height. The sailors would have engaged them in a wrestling match, but FitzRoy put a stop to it fearing that things would get too rough.

Jemmy Button, from his slightly superior perch up the ladder of civilisation, was embarrassed by these antics, and Fuegia Basket ran away. These particular tribesmen, Jemmy explained, were not his own; they were a bad lot, very primitive. FitzRoy was keeping a close eye on Matthews to see what his reactions were. He was a little gloomy, but said that the savages were 'no worse than he had expected'.

So now they loaded the *Beagle*'s four boats with the London Missionary Society's goods (the sailors laughing somewhat as they handed down the chamber-pots), and set off up the quiet waters of the Beagle Channel for Jemmy's own country, Ponsonby Sound. Miraculously the weather cleared, and a bright sun shone on this pristine world of sparkling snowfields and forests. As they approached the Sound they were loudly hailed from the shore, and a fleet of canoes came out to meet them. Presently they arrived at a snug cove, with a delightful meadow dotted with flowers running back into the forest, and here they decided to establish the new settlement. It must have been a strange and pleasant

Darwin's tanager (*Tanagra darwini*), by John Gould.

OPPOSITE Man from Christmas Sound, Tierra del Fuego. ABOVE The crew of the *Beagle* hailed by Fuegians of Jemmy Button's tribe. BELOW Bivouac near Ponsonby Sound. 'Jemmy was now in a district well-known to him, and guided by boats to a quiet, pretty cove named Woollya, surrounded by islets . . .'¹

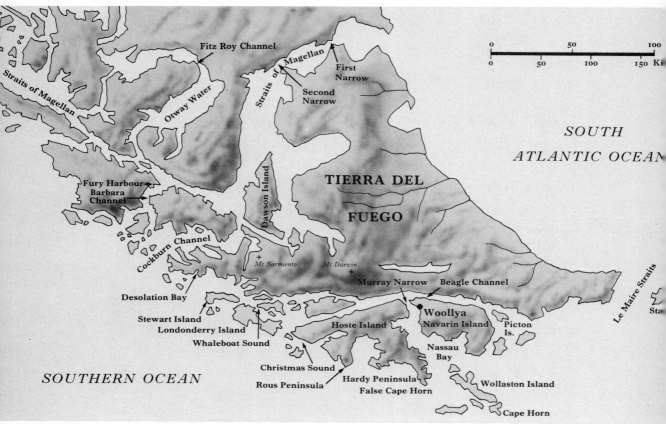

Map of Tierra del Fuego.

scene: the wild Fuegians, numbering a hundred or so, standing apart and watching intently as tents were put up to house the cargo, and the sailors falling to work erecting three wigwams, one for the missionary (who seems to have taken part in the proceedings in a bemused and non-committal way – no doubt he was bottling up his apprehensions), another for Jemmy, and a third for York Minster and Fuegia Basket. The women of the tribe were particularly kind to Fuegia.

Next the digging and planting of a vegetable garden was begun, and in the evening, when the sailors stripped to the waist to wash, the natives stood round them hardly knowing what to marvel at most – the act of washing or the whiteness of their skins. At night they all sat together round the campfires, the sailors shivering in the bitter cold, the Fuegians sweating in the heat of the fire.

The *Beagle* at the foot of Mount Sarmiento.

There was a constrained moment when Jemmy's mother, two sisters and four brothers arrived; the women ran off and hid themselves when they caught sight of Jemmy standing there grandly in his button boots and English suit. He had entirely forgotten his own language; 'It was laughable, but almost pitiable, to hear him speak to his wild brother in English, and then ask him in Spanish whether he did not understand him.' The brothers said nothing; they circled round him like dogs meeting one another for the first time. Next day, however, he clothed them all and things were more friendly.

After five days FitzRoy decided to leave Matthews and his charges to their own devices for a while, and he set off exploring along the Beagle Channel. The scenery was inexpressibly grand. Glaciers reaching down to the indigo sea shone with a translucent blue, and the little boats crept

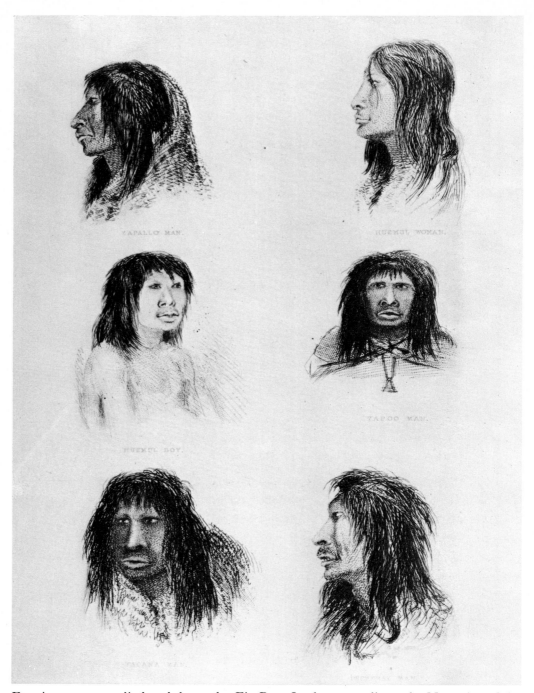

Fuegian types, studied and drawn by FitzRoy. In the appendix to the Narrative of the voyage, FitzRoy included a detailed vocabulary of the various Fuegian dialects.

along under vast mountain ranges and precipices of ice. They found a camping place on a spit of land under a particularly lofty peak that soared up some seven thousand feet directly from the sea, and here they beached their boats and lit a fire. There was a glacier close by with an overhanging cliff, and FitzRoy and Darwin walked up to it to admire the colours of the ice. As they did so a great chunk split off and fell into the sea with a thundering crash that echoed round the mountains. At once a great wave swept down the channel, dashing over the spit of land and tossing their boats about like bits of straw. It was a precarious moment; they were a hundred miles away from the *Beagle,* and had the boats and their stores been washed out to sea they would have been utterly stranded. Darwin was very prompt. With a couple of sailors he ran across two hundred yards of beach and secured the moorings while a second and a third wave crashed over them. FitzRoy was grateful; he named the peak under which they were encamped Mount Darwin.

Darwin had never thought that FitzRoy's experiment with the wild Fuegians had the ghost of a chance of success. He neither liked nor trusted them. After the first contact they had become more and more demanding; 'yammerschooner' was their word when they wanted any-thing, a knife, a handkerchief, a blanket, and before long they had been 'yammerschoonering' all the time and growing increasingly aggressive. Bynoe had witnessed an act of cruelty which had appalled him. A Fuegian child had dropped a basket of seagull eggs, and the wretched child's father, in a fit of rage, had dashed him against the stones again and again until, battered and bleeding, he was abandoned to die.

Jemmy Button had told Darwin that the Fuegians were cannibals — sometimes during a hard winter they would kill and eat their women — and Darwin repeats a conversation which the captain of a sealing ship had with a Fuegian boy. Why, the captain wanted to know, did the Fuegians not eat dogs? 'Dog catch otter', the boy replied, 'women good for nothing; men very hungry'. Real, live cannibals, what were they going to think of this back at The Mount and Maer Hall? 'I feel', Darwin wrote to his sister Caroline, 'quite a disgust at the very sound of the voices of these miserable savages'.

FitzRoy on his side did considerable research on the habits of the Fuegians, particularly the Tekeenica tribe from the south eastern part of Tierra del Fuego, whom he described as 'satires upon mankind . . . the miserable lords of this miserable land'. They had small distorted bodies, caused by their habit of squatting in small wigwams and canoes. The women combed their hair with the jaw of a porpoise; 'about four feet and some inches is the structure of these she-Fuegians – by courtesy called women'. They were the colour of very old mahogany; 'Their rough, coarse and extremely dirty black hair hides yet heightens a villainous expression of the worst description of savage features'.

Thus it was not altogether a surprise when they got back to the camp and found that during the ten days they had been away the natives had overrun the place. Matthews came out to meet them in a state of great agitation. He had a terrible story to tell. Directly the *Beagle* party had gone off the natives had started to pilfer his belongings, and when he had tried to protect them he had been grabbed, knocked down and threatened with death. The vegetable garden had been trampled – the Fuegians had simply laughed when he and Jemmy had tried to stop them – and every day the situation had grown more menacing. Jemmy had been molested as well, but the taciturn York Minster had sided with the natives and had been left alone; and it was strange that little Fuegia Basket now refused even to come out of her hut and greet her friends from the *Beagle*. She wanted nothing to do with white men any more.

FitzRoy was hurt, shocked and bewildered. He had meant these people no wrong, he had only wished to help. Why should they do this to him? Yet he would not give up hope just yet. Matthews, certainly, he would take back on board, but the others must remain and try to make their savage countrymen see the light. He distributed axes to the sullen groups of Fuegians who were standing about, commended Jemmy and York Minster to God, and sailed away, promising to return.

In fact it was a year before he returned. Towards the end of February 1833 they sailed north-east again, stopping at the Falkland islands for a short time. FitzRoy thought them to be admirably suited for a penal establishment, 'a thorough convict colony . . . fully supplied with necessaries yet without luxuries'. It was here that Hellyer, clerk to FitzRoy on the *Beagle*, was drowned while duck-shooting. He had been anxious to shoot some of a kind he had never seen before, and so set off alone with his gun. When he did not return a party set out from the *Beagle* to look for him, and Bynoe found him dead, entangled underwater in the weeds of a creek about a mile away from the ship.

A man of the Tekeenica tribe. 'Their colour is that of very old mahogany, or rather between dark copper and bronze. The trunk of the body is large, in proportion to their cramped and rather crooked limbs.' [N]

ABOVE Fuegian wigwams at Hope Harbour in the Magdalen channel. BELOW Jemmy
Button (LEFT) and his wife in 1834. 'It was indeed Jemmy Button – but how altered! . . .
his hair was long and matted . . . he was wretchedly thin, and his eyes were affected by
smoke.' [N]

After this the *Beagle* set off for a further survey of the Argentinian coast and Darwin made two great journeys inland, but the end of the Fuegian story can be conveniently related here. When the *Beagle* returned a year later the camp was derelict. York Minster and Fuegia had long since decamped with Jemmy's goods and had joined the wild Fuegians. Jemmy himself remained, but he had cast civilisation away as though he had never known it existed; his European clothes had been replaced with a loincloth, he was terribly thin, and his once sleek hair fell in a coarse mat about his painted face. 'We could hardly recognise poor Jemmy', said Darwin; 'Instead of the clean, well-dressed stout lad we left him, we found him a naked thin squalid savage'.

Yet he was friendly; he came out to the *Beagle* in a canoe with a gift of otter skins for FitzRoy and Bynoe and two spearheads for Darwin, and had a meal on board; 'he ate his dinner as tidily as formerly'. But no, he declared, he would not rejoin them. He had found a wife (she kept calling for him from the canoe but would not come on board), these were his people, this was his home, he was finished with civilisation for ever. With all his plans in ruins FitzRoy did what he could to save at least this one soul. He pleaded with Jemmy, he passed down gifts of shawls and a gold-laced cap to his queer little wife in the canoe, but Jemmy was adamant. He paddled back to the shore and the last they saw of him was a dark figure standing there in the light of a campfire waving, as Darwin puts it, 'a long farewell'.

Whatever FitzRoy read into all this, to Darwin at least the facts were clear. Harm rather than good had been done by taking the Fuegians to England; their brief peep at civilisation had merely made it more difficult for them to live in their own country. One could not interrupt the course of nature in this way and hope to succeed. The whole point about primitive races was that they could survive only if they were left alone and were free to adjust themselves to their own environment. If you interfered with them they died. The Red Indians in America were dying, so were the aborigines in Australia; the turn of the Fuegians would come soon enough. By the end of the nineteenth century the three Fuegian tribes were almost extinct. The Alacalufes, canoe people of the Western channels, numbered ten thousand at the time of Darwin's visit; by 1960 there were hardly a hundred.

Soldiers of the east bank of the Plata. Darwin said of General Rosas's own soldiers: 'I should think that such a villainous, banditti-like army, was never before collected together.' [J]

CHAPTER VI

THE PAMPAS

One begins to notice a hardening, an increasing tension in FitzRoy's nature from this point onwards. The more his plans miscarry, the greater the difficulties that mount up before him, the more determined he becomes. He does not lose touch with the feelings of his crew—this man could never be a Captain Bligh—but the generous, kindly side of his nature tends to become overshadowed in his persistent hunt for perfection. He was a superb cartographer, but it was a fearfully difficult business trying to chart the South American coast in storms that hardly ever ceased, too much for one ship to accomplish. Well then, he decides, he will acquire additional vessels to help him carry out the work. No time to consult the Admiralty over this important step; he will take the money out of his own pocket and they can refund him later on.

And so he begins by chartering and manning two small boats and ends up by buying outright, for £1300, an American sealing vessel of 170 tons, almost as big as the *Beagle* herself. He renames her the *Adventure*: 'I had often anxiously longed for a consort, adapted for carrying cargoes, rigged up so as to be easily worked with few hands, and able to keep company with the *Beagle*'. He has to recondition this ship, he has to run the *Beagle* back and forth between Montevideo and the Patagonian coast in order to victual his little fleet, but nothing matters so long as the work progresses. Thus the next eighteen months were for FitzRoy a time of very great strain, and as he grows thin and nervous from overwork he retreats, as it were, upon himself.

With Darwin it is altogether different. By now (the spring of 1833), he knows the ropes, the last remnants of his hesitancy and inexperience drop away and he becomes a very useful member of the expedition. The idea of his entering the church grew fainter and fainter, and natural history possessed him entirely. 'There is nothing like geology', he wrote to Catherine; 'The pleasure of the first day's partridge shooting or the first day's hunting cannot be compared to finding a fine group of fossil bones, which tell their story of former times with almost a living tongue . . . I collect every living creature which I have time to catch and preserve'. In his journals which he kept up faithfully day by day one can see his confidence steadily increasing; his ideas form patterns and speculations begin to harden into theories.

In May, when the *Beagle* went off on survey, Darwin was landed at Maldonado, a quiet forlorn little town at the entrance of the Rio Plata, and here he stayed for ten weeks making a collection of mammals, birds and reptiles. During this time he made a two weeks' trip into the interior, as far as the river Polanco, 70 miles away. The state of the country was such that he was forced to take two armed men with him, and twelve horses; only the week before a traveller from Montevideo had been found dead on the road. They stayed in the house of Don Manuel Fuentes, a rich land-owner, where Darwin was considered to be extremely eccentric, if not actually mad. 'People look at me rather kindly but with much pity and wonder . . . I am considered such a curiosity that I was sent to be shown to a sick woman.' The whole family collected to see the wonders of his compass and match-box.

When he got back to Maldonado he spent several weeks parcelling up bones, rocks, plants, skins of birds and other creatures to be sent home. In one of his notebooks he catalogued fifteen hundred and twenty-nine specimens, from fishes to fungi, sent home in spirits of wine. 'My collection of the birds and quadrupeds of this place is becoming very perfect. A few Reales has enlisted all the boys in the town in my service, and few days pass in which they do not bring me some curious creature.' It was not always easy for Henslow at the other end to know what he was getting. 'For goodness' sake what is no. 233?' he wrote once. 'It looks like the remains of an electric explosion, a mere mass of soot—something very curious I daresay.'

At the end of July the *Beagle* picked Darwin up at Maldonado and sailed for El Carmen in Patagonia. He was now ready to set off on the first of his great inland journeys. El Carmen, about 18 miles upstream from the mouth of the Rio Negro, was the most southerly outpost inhabited by civilised people on the American continent. Buenos Aires lay some 600 miles to the north, and all the intervening plain—the Pampas— was unexplored territory over which tribes of wild Indians roamed and

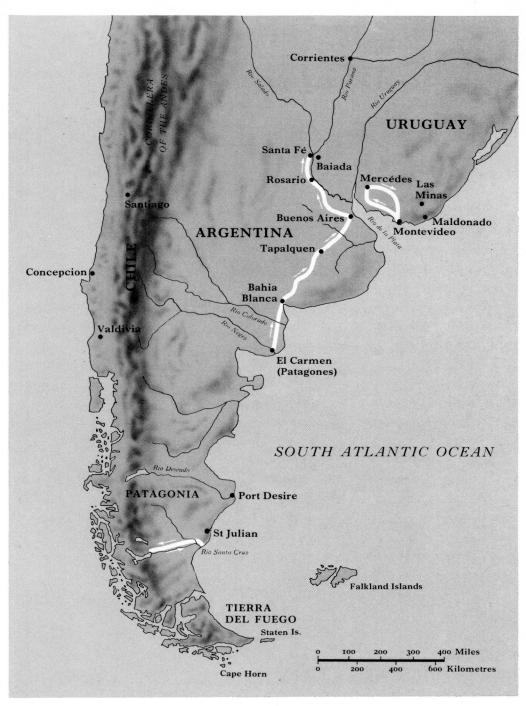

Map of the east coast of South America.

hunted. They were fierce and aggressive people when aroused and great horsemen; they kept to their primitive beliefs and thought that the stars were old Indians, the Milky Way the field where the old Indians hunt ostriches and the Magellan clouds the feathers of the ostriches they kill. Just now they were fighting for their lives against the Argentinians who wanted their lands in order to graze their expanding herds of cattle; in fact, it was the story of the American Middle West all over again, except that here the struggle was even more primitive and ruthless. The Indians were of course fighting a losing battle against a war of extermination; once there had been villages of two to three thousand of them, but by the time of Darwin's visit the tribes now mostly wandered homeless across the Pampas.

General Rosas, the commander of the Argentinian forces, had established himself about 80 miles north of El Carmen on the Rio Colorado, where he was close to Bahia Blanca, the place where Darwin had found his prehistoric bones and the only other civilised settlement in the area. From the Rio Colorado Rosas had a tenuous line of supply, a string of lightly manned outposts, leading all the way back to Buenos Aires. Apart from these outposts—or *postas*, merely tiny dots in the vast plain—the whole

The village of El Carmen in Patagonia.

region was a no man's land where the Indians made spasmodic raids on travellers whenever and wherever they could.

Darwin's plan was to ride overland from El Carmen to the Rio Colorado, make contact with Rosas and then push on from *posta* to *posta* all the way to Buenos Aires. He wanted to do this partly one suspects for the adventure of the thing, but ostensibly because this was the only way he could really investigate the geology and the flora and fauna of the Pampas. FitzRoy, himself an adventurer and explorer, approved of the plan; indeed it must have given him some pleasure to see how the eager and inexperienced young man he had recruited in London two years before had turned himself into this self-reliant campaigner who was apparently willing to go anywhere and do anything in the interests of science and religion—yes, certainly religion; who knew what revelations of Biblical truth might not be discovered in that vast unknown hinterland? But first there must be a few reasonable precautions; Darwin must have a guide and a small body-guard, and it was arranged that the *Beagle* should make a rendezvous with him at Bahia Blanca, 500 miles away. Then if all was well Darwin could ride on again to Buenos Aires.

An Englishman named Harris, owner of one of FitzRoy's schooners,

Toldo [hut] and tomb of Patagonian Indians.

was living at El Carmen, and he volunteered to act as a guide as far as the Colorado. An escort of six gauchos was hired, and on 11 August Darwin said goodbye to his companions on the *Beagle* and set off. Their way at first lay across the desert, and it was astonishing that the waterless plain could support so many different birds and other creatures. An ostrich—properly named a *Rhea*, smaller than the African bird—would start up in front of them, its wings outspread as it raced away, and off they would go in pursuit with the *bolas* (the weapon of the gauchos, to be explained later) whistling through the air; for Darwin it was like his hunting days all over again. He was particularly interested in these ostriches; flocks of as many as twenty to thirty birds were seen 'presenting a very noble appearance' against a clear sky; 'it was easy to gallop up within a short distance of them; but then, expanding their wings they made all sail right before the wind, and soon left the horse astern'. In a different sort of country they took readily to water; later on the Santa Cruz river Darwin twice saw them swimming across the river at a point where its course was rapid and 400 yards wide. 'When swimming, very little of their bodies appear above water; their necks are extended a little forward, and their progress is slow.'

Their nesting habits were unusual: several hens used the same nest, which sometimes had as many as seventy or eighty eggs in it, though more generally twenty or thirty. The cock bird did the sitting and hatching, and if it was disturbed on a nest could be very savage, and would chase a man on horseback. The males were easily distinguished from the females, not only by their darker colour and bigger head, but by the noise they made, 'a singular, deep-toned hissing note; when first I heard it, standing in the midst of some sand-hillocks, I thought it was made by some wild beast, for it is a sound that one cannot tell whence it comes, or from how far distant'. One example of a special species, rare and wary by nature, was caught by Darwin and sent back to the Zoological Society; later it was named after him, *Rhea darwini*.

Once the gauchos ran down a puma and roasted its veal-like flesh over an open fire; and usually there were deer or guanacos to shoot. They were accompanied on their hunting forays by vultures and eagles who were always attracted by the sight of blood, sometimes from many miles away. With claws out-thrust and the hooked beak jutting out between two murderous eyes the birds would swoop down upon a carcass and within a few minutes pick it to the bones. They would take a man if they could get him. 'A person', Darwin wrote, 'will discover the necrophagous habits of the Carrancha (Caracara) by walking out on one of the desolate plains, and lying down to sleep. When he awakes he will see, on each surrounding hillock, one of these birds patiently watching him with an evil eye'. These unattractive birds had truly disgusting habits. They hung around slaughter-houses, picked at the sores on the horses' backs, and watched for a sheep to give birth so as to kill the young lamb.

The smaller animals were fascinating; skunks or zorillos came wandering confidently by, casting out their outrageous smell on the evening air, a smell which can be perceived as far as a league away; 'certain it is that every animal willingly makes room for the zorillo'. The little mole-like tuco-tuco emitted piercing disembodied screams from its burrow; 'it may be briefly described as a Gnawer'. Its name comes from the short repeated grunt which it makes underground; when angry or frightened the tuco-tucos are incessant. The gentle armadillo was always

LEFT The pichiciego, a species of armadillo. 'The instant one was perceived, it was necessary, in order to catch it, almost to tumble off one's horse; for in soft soil the animal burrowed so quickly, that its hinder quarters would almost disappear before one could alight.'[1] RIGHT *Rhea darwini*. Darwin was told of this rare species by the Gauchos: 'they said its colour was dark and mottled and that its legs were shorter and feathered lower down than those of the common ostrich . . . Mr Gould in describing this new species, has done me the honour of calling it after my name'.[1]

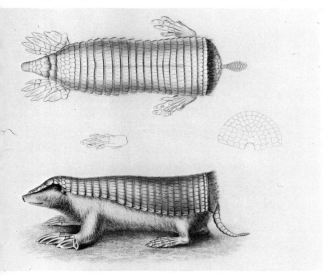

ABOVE Estancia on the Rio San Pedro. BELOW Herd of cattle crossing a river.

too quick for Darwin; he could never get off his horse before it had dug itself into the sand. 'It seems almost a pity to kill such nice little animals', said one of the gauchos as he sharpened his knife on the back of one, 'they are so quiet'. Armadillo was particularly good to eat if it was roasted in its shell. Then, as they advanced into better country, they came on partridges and black-necked swans, and flamingos that cast long reflections of bright pink in the water-holes in the early morning light.

All this time Darwin was taking intensely detailed notes on the birds, their habits, their flight, their eggs, their songs: 'infinitely sweet . . . Bird runs like animal at bottom of hedge, does not easily fly, not loud . . . long-legged plover cry like little dog's hunting bark'. He was already getting that devotion to work, the habit of ceaseless industry, which made him write later: 'I trust that I shall act—as I now think—that a man who dares to waste one hour of time, has not discovered the value of life . . . there is nothing as intolerable as idleness'. An entry in his notebook for 17 August 1833 reads: 'A day spent in killing time [they were held up by rain] . . . no books . . . I envied the very kittens playing on the mud floor'. He could not stand inaction of any sort. 4 September: 'Cruel ennui . . . found books exquisite delight'. October: 'Ennui—yellow-breasted bird . . . sings well'.

They stayed a night at an *estancia* belonging to an Englishman, and Darwin studied the curious method of rearing the sheep-dogs which could be seen guarding large flocks of sheep at great distances from the house. These were trained by being separated from their mothers while still small puppies and put to live with the sheep. 'An ewe is held three or four times a day for the little thing to suck, and a nest of wool made for it in the sheep pen; at no time is it allowed to associate with other dogs, or with the children of the family.' Very often the puppy was castrated too, so once it was adult it had no desire to leave the flock, and just as an ordinary dog will defend its master, man, so would these dogs defend the sheep. The flocks were seldom attacked, even by the hungry wild dogs, who somehow seemed to confuse the dog with the sheep, and would not after all take on a flock of sheep-dogs.

Generally by night the party camped around a fire on the open plain, their saddles for pillows and their saddle-cloths for blankets, and the scene for Darwin had a kind of magic: the horses tethered on the edge of the firelight, the remains of their dinner, an ostrich or a deer, strewn

Method of throwing: LEFT The *lazo*. 'The Gaucho, when he is going to use the lazo, keeps a small coil in his bridle-hand, and in the other holds the running noose, which is made very large, generally having a diameter of about eight feet.' RIGHT The *bolas*. 'The Gaucho holds the smallest of the three [balls] in his hand, and whirls the other two round and round his head; then, taking aim, sends them like chain shot revolving through the air.'[1]

about on the ground, the tuco-tuco uttering its subterranean grunt, the men smoking cigars and playing cards, the dogs keeping watch, and all pausing if an unfamiliar noise came to them out of the darkness. They would place their ears to the ground and listen intently; one never knew just how or when the Indians would attack.

Darwin loved the gauchos. They were as tough and leathery as old boots. Even in that untrammelled age they were wildly picturesque men with their moustachios and long black hair falling down over their shoulders. They wore scarlet ponchos and wide riding drawers, white boots with huge spurs, and knives stuck into their waistbands. They were extremely polite and looked, Darwin said, 'as if they would cut your throat and make a bow at the same time'. Meat was their diet, nothing but meat, and they used the bones of the animals as fuel for their cooking fires. They had a peculiar method of hunting. All the men would disperse in different directions, and then at an appointed time (accurate by guesswork, they had no way of telling the time), they would meet together and drive all the animals they had mustered into some central spot and there kill them.

When they were not hunting they liked to play the guitar, to smoke, and occasionally engage in a little drunken brawling with their knives. They were superb horsemen; the idea of being thrown in any circumstances never entered their head. Like skaters on thin ice, they galloped at full speed over ground so rough that it would have been impassable at a slower pace. They forced their horses to swim great rivers; a man, naked, would ride his horse into the water, and once out of its depth he would slip off its back and catch hold of its tail. Each time the horse tried to turn back the man splashed water in its face and drove it on—thus he was towed across to the other side.

Their hunting weapon was the *bolas*, two or three stones tied at the end of leather thongs which were whirled round the head and hurled at the animal they were pursuing in such a way that its legs became entangled and it was thrown to the ground. They had learnt this as children by practising with miniature *bolas* on dogs, and it was usually done at full gallop; Darwin, trying it at a trot, gave great pleasure to the gauchos by bringing down his own horse and himself with it.

On the third day they crossed the Rio Colorado where a great troop of

A horse race.

mares—the soldiers' food when they were on the march—was being swum across the stream. Darwin found it a ludicrous spectacle: 'Hundreds and hundreds of heads, all directed one way, with pointed ears and distended snorting nostrils, appearing just above the water like a great shoal of some amphibious animals'. He was told that these horses could travel a hundred miles a day.

In the evening they arrived at General Rosas's camp. The place looked more like the hide-out of a band of brigands than the headquarters of an invading army. Guns, wagons and crude straw huts had been formed into a sort of compound, 400 yards square, and within it the general's rough and ready cavalrymen were encamped. Many of them were of mixed Indian, negro and Spanish blood, others were Indian tribesmen who had come over to the Argentinian side, and in addition there were camp followers galore: rather splendid-looking Indian women with gaudy dresses and black plaits hanging down their backs, who rode their horses with their knees hunched up high; theirs was the job of carrying the soldiers' kit on the baggage animals, of making camp and cooking the food. Dogs and cattle roamed about in the dust.

The general himself was as horsy and flamboyant as his men. He kept in his entourage a couple of buffoons for his amusement, and he was reputed to be most dangerous when he laughed; those were the moments when he was liable to order a man to be shot or perhaps tortured by being suspended by his arms and legs from four posts driven into the ground. They had a test of horsemanship on the Pampas. A man would perch himself on a crossbar above the entrance to a corral, and when a wild horse, both bridle-less and unsaddled, was driven out the man would drop on to the beast's back and ride it until it came to a standstill. Rosas could perform this feat. He was also, however, a man of authority; later on he was destined to be dictator of Argentina for many years. He welcomed Darwin very gravely and courteously to his camp and Darwin was evidently charmed. He wrote that the general would use his influence for the advancement and prosperity of the country – a prophecy which, as he himself was forced to admit ten years later, turned out 'entirely and miserably wrong'. Rosas became a great tyrant.

The tactics of his campaign against the Indians were really quite simple; he was rounding up the stragglers on the Pampas, small tribes of a hundred or so who lived close to the *salinas* or salt lakes, and when

116   ABOVE Hunting ostriches with the *bolas*. BELOW Gauchos at a camp fire. OVERLEAF The *Beagle* in Murray Narrow, Beagle Channel. Watercolour by Conrad Martens.

those that escaped him had all been driven into one place he proposed to massacre the lot. There was not much chance of any Indians escaping south over the Rio Negro, he explained, as he had an arrangement with a friendly tribe there by which they agreed to murder any fugitives who came their way. They were quite eager to do this, Rosas said, because he had told them that he would shoot one of their own people for every enemy Indian who managed to escape.

The camp during Darwin's stay was in a continual uproar, with news and rumours of skirmishes coming in by the hour. One day it was reported that one of Rosas's outposts on the route to Buenos Aires had been wiped out, and a commandant named Miranda was ordered to go out with three hundred men and take reprisals. 'They passed the night here', Darwin relates (he was visiting Bahia Blanca, which was close by, at the time), 'and it was impossible to conceive anything more wild and savage than the scene of their bivouac. Some drank until they were intoxicated; others swallowed the steaming blood of the cattle slaughtered for their suppers; and then, being sick from drunkenness, they cast it up again, and were besmeared with filth and gore'.

In the morning the men set off for the scene of the murder, with orders to follow the *rastro* or track even if it led them to Chile. They were expert at deciphering a track; from examining the prints of a thousand horses they could tell how many were mounted, how many loaded; even, by the unevenness of the hoof marks, how tired they were. 'These men would penetrate to the end of the world', says Darwin. He heard later that the raid was successful. A party of Indians had been sighted travelling across the open plain, and Miranda's men had charged them at the gallop. The Indians had had no time to put up a concerted defence, they fled in different directions, each individual trying to save himself. Some of the fugitives when cornered were very fierce; one dying man had bitten his assailant's thumb and would not let go even when his eye was forced out. Another man who was wounded pretended to be dead and then sprang forward with his knife upon one of the soldiers. A third man pleaded for mercy but was observed to be loosening the *bolas* round his waist so as to be ready to strike when his pursuer came close. His throat was cut. In the end some hundred and ten men, women and children were rounded up. All the men who were not likely to be useful as informants were shot. The better-looking girls were set aside to be distributed among

Three species of Argentinian palm-trees: *Cocos yatai, Cocos australis, Copernica cerifera.*

121

General Rosas. One of his buffoons said of him: 'when the general laughs, he spares neither mad man nor sound . . .'[J]

the soldiers later on, and the older women and the uglier girls were then murdered. The children were taken off to be sold as slaves.

Among the prisoners who were spared there were three particularly fine-looking young men, all very fair and over six foot in height. They were lined up for interrogation and when the first refused to divulge the whereabouts of the rest of the tribe he was shot dead. So was the second, and the third had no hesitation either: 'Fire', he said, 'I am a man. I can die'. Vultures, being familiar with these scenes, hovered overhead.

Darwin was horrified, but there was little he could do except confide to his diary the thought that these Christian soldiers were much more savage than the helpless pagans they were destroying. Yet everyone in Rosas's camp was convinced that what they were doing was absolutely justified and right. The Indians had resented the Argentinians over-running their hunting grounds and had slaughtered the ranchers' sheep and cattle. Therefore they were criminals and had to be destroyed. Let Darwin himself get caught by them and he would find out just how gentle they were. At least, he argued, the women might be spared, but it was explained to him: 'You can't keep them. They breed so fast'. In brief, the Indians were vermin, worse than rats, and that was that.

Among the women captured in this raid were two very pretty Spanish girls who had been kidnapped as children by the Indians – this war had been going on for a long time – and had been brought up by them. They had forgotten their native tongue, had become completely native in their ways, and were now facing the prospect of re-adjusting themselves to civilisation, which probably meant concubinage and semi-enslavement among Rosas's drunken, hard-bitten cavalrymen.

This then was the brutal war that the grave and courteous General Rosas was carrying on against the natives of Patagonia, and it seemed to Darwin that it could only end in one way; the retreat of the survivors to the more inaccessible mountains and eventually the extermination of the race; a very practical application of the theory of the survival of the fittest. What chance would there be for the Fuegians when their turn came?

Darwin himself had a scare one day. He was riding out from Bahia Blanca with a couple of gauchos when they caught sight of three horsemen in the distance. 'They don't ride like Christians', one of the gauchos said, and it was decided to make towards a nearby swamp where they could hide. Darwin loaded his pistols and they made off, galloping over the uneven ground when they were out of sight of the strangers and walking (so as to pretend they were not frightened) when they came into view again. They halted when they got to the foot of a hill, their dogs were made to lie down, and one of the gauchos crawled forward on his hands and knees to reconnoitre. At the top of the rise he gazed intently at the enemy for a moment and burst out laughing: '*Mugeres*' – it was three women, the wives of some of Rosas's officers, out hunting for ostrich eggs.

The *Beagle* turned up in Bahia Blanca on 24 August and Darwin went on board and spent the entire day relating his adventures to FitzRoy. FitzRoy seems to have been a good listener, and Darwin was eloquent; he had no difficulty in persuading FitzRoy to allow him to continue on the second and longer leg of his journey, 400 miles through uninhabited country, even though from now on he would be without Harris and alone with the gauchos.

There was a wonderful exuberance about these days, a sense of freedom that was heightened by the element of risk. 'There is high enjoyment in the independence of the gaucho life – to be able at any moment to pull up your horse and say, "Here we will pass the night".' As Darwin rode on to Buenos Aires even the gauchos were astonished at his energy. If he saw a mountain he had to climb it – and he was probably the first European to ascend the 3500-foot Sierra de la Ventana. When he reached the top he found it broken in half by a valley. He crossed it, climbed again, and reached the second peak with great difficulty: 'Every 20 yards I had the cramp in the upper part of both thighs, so that I was afraid I should not have been able to have got down again'. But when one of the gauchos' horses went lame Darwin gave the man his own horse and walked. Gauchos, he explained later, could not walk. He smoked his cigar, drank his *maté,* and thrived on a diet of solid meat, broken once only by a lucky find of an ostrich's nest with twenty-seven eggs in it, each egg eleven times the weight of a hen's egg. Once he went twenty hours without water.

By the campfire at night he read a little from the copy of Milton's *Paradise Lost* which he always carried with him and wrote up his notes on the day's adventures. They were not dull: 'Night at Sierra very cold, first wet with dew, then frozen stiff . . . saw beautiful oriole . . .Foxes in immense numbers. Found one little toad, most singular from its colour (black and vermillion) thinking to give it a great treat carried it to a pool of water; not only was the little animal unable to swim, but I think without help it would have drowned. . . . Many snakes with black patches in deep swamp, 2 yellow lines and red tail . . . lake enlivened by many black-necked swans and beautiful ducks and cranes . . . last night remarkable hailstorm (deer, 20 hides) already found dead and about 15 ostriches . . . hailstones as big as apples . . . slept at house of half mad-man . . . Indians going to *salinas* for salt – eat salt like sugar . . . women taken prisoners at 20 years never content . . . wife of old caique not more than 11 . . . ostriches lay eggs in middle of day . . . cranes carry bundles of rushes . . .'

So it goes on day after day, and he never seems to be tired, never loses his curiosity or his sense of wonder. Finally after forty days in the wilderness we find him riding into Buenos Aires through orchards of quinces and peaches, and with his beard, his wide hat, his worn clothes and his sunburnt face he must have looked like some cowboy, or perhaps a gold prospector coming into town after a hard spell on the trail. He was leathery and as horny as the gauchos themselves.

The black-necked swan (*Cygnus nigricollis*), often encountered by Darwin on the lakes and in the swamps of Argentina.

A Spanish lady with the close-fitting gown and black silk veil, which made Darwin write to his sisters: 'I am sorry for you all. It would do the whole tribe of you a great deal of good to come to Buenos Aires'.

CHAPTER VII

BUENOS AIRES

Buenos Aires had its charms. 'Our chief amusement', Darwin wrote to his sisters, 'was riding about and admiring the Spanish ladies. After watching one of these angels gliding down the streets, involuntarily we groaned out, "How foolish English women are, they can neither walk nor dress". And then how ugly *Miss* sounds after *Signorita* . . . One never saw one of their charming backs without crying out "How beautiful she must be".'

The caballeros of Buenos Aires were evidently of the same mind. Darwin was approached one day by a captain in the army who said he had a question to ask. 'It was "Whether the ladies of Buenos Aires were not the handsomest in the world". I replied, "Charmingly so". He added, "I have one other question: Do ladies in any other part of the world wear such large combs?" I solemnly assured him they did not. They were absolutely delighted. The captain exclaimed, "Look there, a man who has seen half the world, says it is the case; we always thought so, but now we know it" '.

Darwin returned to this theme later on when he reached Lima in Peru: 'The close elastic gown fits the figure closely and obliges the ladies to walk with very small steps, which they do very elegantly, and display very white silk stockings and very pretty feet. They wear a black silk veil which is fixed round the waist behind and brought over the head and held by the hands before the face, allowing only one eye to remain uncovered. But then that one is so black and brilliant and has such powers of motion and expression, that its effect is very powerful. Altogether the ladies are so metamorphised that I at first felt as much surprised as if I had been introduced amongst a number of nice round mermaids. I could not keep my eyes away from them.'

But this apparently was as far as he got. In Buenos Aires he lived at the home of a Mr Lumb who was a respectable English resident (Mrs

Lumb reminded Darwin of England when she poured the tea), and he was much too busy to get entangled. There were a number of English stores in the town and he shopped with abandon: writing paper, pens, beeswax and resin, mousetraps and glass jars for his specimens, powder and balls for his pistols, a pair of trousers for Covington (who rejoined him at Buenos Aires), and for himself stockings, gloves, handkerchiefs, a night cap, cigars and snuff. One shopping list read: 'Paper . . .scizzors, dentist, watch mended . . . spurs . . . French dentist . . . cigars . . . dentist . . . animal without tail . . . bookseller'. Clearly he was suffering from toothache, but what was the animal without a tail? In addition to all these he wrote home urgently for '4 pairs of very strong walking shoes from Howell's', new lenses for his microscope, and books, above all scientific books.

Then there were his specimens to pack up and send to Henslow; two hundred skins of birds and other creatures, fish, insects, mice, stones, 'a fine set of fossil bones', and many exotic seeds which he hoped could be made to grow in England. The question of money was a nagging business; his shore excursions were proving expensive and he had already overspent his allowance. Now, as he drew a bill for another £80, he winced at the thought of what Dr Darwin was going to say; he trusted, he wrote to his sisters, that his father 'after his first great growl' was over, would not grudge the money; surely he would understand that this voyage was changing his life, that he would never be able to return here, that he must see everything there was to be seen no matter what the cost. 'I wish', he wrote home, 'the same feeling did not act so strongly on the Captain. He is eating an enormous hole into his capital for the sake of advancing all the objects of the voyage . . . [he] asked me if I could pay a year in advance for my mess. I did so . . . for I could not refuse to a person who is so systematically munificent to everyone who approaches him'.

There was another reason for Darwin to feel guilty when he thought of his father; sooner or later he would have to tell him that he would never now go into the Church. But for the moment he dodged this issue; in his letters home he never mentions the matter of his future – it is only the present that counts.

Darwin did not really like Buenos Aires. During the next four months while he was waiting for the *Beagle* to complete her Patagonian survey he got away on excursions whenever he could. He thought the plazas

The *matadero,* or public butcheries, 'where the animals are kept for slaughter to supply food to this beef-eating population'.

and the wide streets very fine, and he enjoyed doing the sights: the theatres (where the men sat in the pit and women in the gallery), the museums, and the great corral where the animals for slaughter were kept, 'one of the spectacles best worth seeing'. A man on horseback threw his lassoo round the horns of a beast and dragged him to the chosen spot where 'the matador with great caution cuts the hamstrings . . . the whole sight is horrible and revolting; the ground is almost made of bones, and the horses and riders are drenched with gore'. In the ornate churches there was, to his low-church protestant eye, perhaps a little too much fervour and a surprising informality among the congregation: 'The Spanish lady with her brilliant shawl kneels by the side of her black servant in the open aisle.'

Village on the Parana river.

But the surrounding countryside was dreary and the perpetual rain depressing. Nor did he think much in general of the inhabitants of Buenos Aires (60,000 of them at this time). The wealthy Creole he openly detested: 'He is a profligate sensualist who laughs at all religion; he is open to the grossest corruption; his want of principle is entire'. Every official from the Chief Justice downwards was bribable.

Darwin was not a prude nor a sentimentalist; without sharing FitzRoy's rigidities he was a fastidious man, an enthusiast with a fairly strict code of manners, and just now, when the world was opening up so wonderfully before him, and was so exciting, he was impatient of all laziness and indifference in other people, and furious at their active cruelty. The voyage had swallowed him up. It was all so new and desperately important. He was genuinely amazed when two of the *Beagle*'s petty officers,

130

who no doubt had had enough of FitzRoy's discipline, deserted from the ship.

Certainly there was no sign in Darwin of the hypochondriac of later years. He was ill with fever during a trip he made to Santa Fé, but he threw this off very easily and except for sea-sickness we never hear him complaining of such minor ailments as toothache, though he must have been suffering from it for some time to judge from his visits to the French dentist in Buenos Aires. His beard was a massive affair, and must have made him look older than his twenty-four years, and now that his Spanish was improving he moved around the town with the air of an experienced traveller: Don Carlos, a young English gentleman of private means. It was always a tremendous joy when letters arrived from his family and from Henslow – he hung upon every word – but there is no sign as yet of homesickness. He wants to go on and on.

His Santa Fé trip, however, was very nearly his undoing. He had arranged to rejoin the *Beagle* before she sailed from Montevideo late in October, and he estimated that this would give him ample time to make the 300 mile ride up to the Parana river, where he had heard that fossil bones were to be found. On 27 September he rode out of Buenos Aires into the Northern Pampas, then breast-high with giant thistles. At first all went well, though the journey was not without risk, since it was a popular route for Indian attacks. At one point they passed the skeleton of an Indian suspended from the branch of a tree, and Darwin's guides viewed the sight with 'much satisfaction'. Close to the pretty provincial town of Santa Fé he found his fossil bones easily enough: a splendid deposit embedded in the river bank. The town itself was a quiet little place, clean and in good order. Its governor was a man whose favourite sport was hunting Indians; not long before he had slaughtered forty-eight, and sold the children off at the rate of three or four pounds each.

But then Darwin went down with fever (probably it was malaria, for he describes how his hands were black with mosquitoes whenever he exposed them), and he was forced to lie in bed for a week while a kindly old woman looked after him. He was offered strange remedies, some harmless, such as a compress of split beans wound round the head, others 'too disgusting to mention'. 'Little hairless dogs', he wrote, 'are in great request to sleep at the feet of invalids'.

When he felt better he decided that it would be quicker to return by river, and so he abandoned his horses and got on board a decrepit trading boat that was sailing to Buenos Aires. It was the most exasperating of journeys. The Argentinian captain was fearful of every breeze that blew and of every current that swirled round the islands, and so they remained anchored to the shore for days on end, and crept downstream only for a few hours at a time. At last ('*Gracias a dios*' exclaims Darwin in his notebook) on 20 October they reached the little village of Las Conchas just outside the capital, and Darwin rushed ashore to find a horse – or canoe – anything to get him into the city. At once he found himself surrounded by armed men who refused to allow him to go on. Revolution had broken out and the city was blockaded.

General Rosas, it seemed, was not only interested in hunting down wild Indians; he was out to overturn the Argentinian government as well. His friends in Buenos Aires had raised the cry of '*Viva Rosas*', and all the surrounding countryside was up in arms. In the city itself the streets were cleared, the shops had pulled down their shutters, bullets were flying about and the general's forces were allowing no one to pass either in or out through the city gates. Frantic with anxiety that he would miss the *Beagle,* Darwin argued and protested, and in the end, after a long ride round the town, managed to reach the camp of Rosas's brother. He explained grandly that he was an intimate and important friend of the general. 'Magic itself', Darwin says, 'could not have altered circumstances quicker'. He was told that he could go on ahead on foot to the city without his baggage if he liked to take the risk of being shot. It was a lonely three-mile walk down the empty road. Once a party of soldiers stopped him, but he showed them an out-of-date passport and they let him continue. Once inside the city among his friends he was safe enough, but his position was hardly improved; Covington was still outside and so were all his clothes and the specimens he had collected on his trip. It was dangerous to move about in the streets since the Government soldiers were using this heaven-sent opportunity to waylay and rob any civilian who came their way.

For a fortnight Darwin fumed and fretted, and it was a situation that had some resemblance to the adventures of Phileas Fogg and Passepartout on their frantic eighty days' journey round the world. Here they were, master and servant, trying to get together, desperate to hurry on, and the whole world apparently conspiring against them. For Darwin the prospect

Approach to Montevideo Bay. Drawing by Conrad Martens who replaced Augustus Earle as the *Beagle's* official artist.

of the *Beagle* sailing away and leaving him stranded in Buenos Aires was too horrible to be thought of. At last he succeeded in bribing a man to go out and bring Covington in. He does not say how it was done – probably it was by night and on horseback with the guards agreeing to look the other way – but at all events Covington arrived and together they managed to get aboard a ship that slipped through the blockade and down the river to Montevideo. The vessel was crammed with refugees who were all sick in the Rio Plata, and Darwin's heart must have given a great bound of relief when he saw at the journey's end the *Beagle's* masts rising placidly at her anchorage in Montevideo Bay.

FitzRoy all this time had been hanging doggedly on to his surveying operations, eating alone in his cabin, obsessed by work, and never for a

Self-portrait by Conrad Martens. FitzRoy said that his great disappointment at losing Earle was 'diminished by meeting Mr Martens at Monte Video, and engaging him to embark with me as my draughtsman'. [N]

moment getting a respite from the responsibility of commanding two
ships. Most of the surveying had to be done from small boats working
close inshore, and usually in rough seas; a dangerous business and a
never-ending anxiety for their commander. Just now he was at work
on his charts collating the many calculations they had made along the
Patagonian coast in the past few months, a tedious and exacting business,
and Darwin, fresh from his adventures on shore, must have seemed to
burst upon him in his cabin with the exuberance of a schoolboy returning
from his holidays. Here were all his wonderful specimens to spread out
on the deck: his prehistoric bones, the skins of many brilliant birds and
other creatures, a spider that spun a web like a sail and flew through the
air, a *bolas* and other native weapons, serpents bottled in alcohol and
parcels of exotic seeds and flowers that were unknown in Europe. Then
too there were all his exploits to recount: the revolution, his journey
down the Parana river, his *tigre* (or jaguar) hunting on the islands; on
the river banks he had seen tree trunks deeply scratched, the marks, so
his guides told him, of the claws of a jaguar. 'I imagine this habit of the
jaguar', he wrote, 'is exactly similar to one which may any day be seen
in the common cat, as with outstretched legs and exserted claws it scrapes
the legs of a chair'. Be that as it may, he told FitzRoy that the fear of
tigres had quite destroyed his pleasure in scrambling through the woods.
He described his gallops with the gauchos, the poor slave-children he
had seen being sold to the debauched grandees of the Pampas, the ladies
of the capital in their mantillas, and the undiscovered mountains that he,
and he alone, had climbed.

FitzRoy must have been something less than human if he did not feel
a pang of envy. He was entertained, no doubt, but one sees that aristocratic eye resting on Darwin a little coldly. Certainly he was to be forgiven
if he found that he had heard enough for the moment, if with some curt
phrase he turned away and told Darwin to get his junk out of the cabin
and stow it, if he fell into one of his 'severe silences', or even if he enquired
of Darwin about just where all these exciting investigations were taking
him – just how far had he succeeded in relating them to the fundamental
truths of the Bible. That surely was important; and it was a calculation
that had to be every bit as precise as the *Beagle*'s charting of the coast.
There was such a thing as not seeing the wood because of the trees.

But Darwin, if we are to trust his notebooks, was not thinking of God at all through these days; he was absorbed in the trees and everything inside the wood, and he was beginning to entertain the notion that truth was not something that was imposed from above, but would be revealed bit by bit by man's own practical researches on this earth. And so he might have been a little crestfallen when the *Beagle*'s discipline and austerity closed round him after his exuberant return. He was back in school again.

By the end of 1833, when Darwin rejoined the ship at Montevideo, the Patagonian survey was all but done. The *Beagle*'s sailors had been more than a year among the storms and the cold of that arid coast, and they were all heartily sick of it. Augustus Earle, the artist, had never been well since he left England, and his health was now so broken that he had to leave the ship. He was replaced by Conrad Martens, 'an excellent landscape drawer . . . a pleasant person, and like all birds of that class, full up to the neck with enthusiasm'. Darwin, for his part, soon parcelled up the last of his Pampas collections for shipment to England and could think of one thing only: the day when they would round the Horn and sail out into the calm sunny waters of the Pacific. Not even the prospect of capturing a live *Megatherium,* he said, could hold him back. By now he had pretty well made up his mind about the geology of the eastern seaboard; it had been raised above the sea, he believed, in fairly recent times. But it was the Andes, with their great volcanoes, that held the real clue to the geology of the peninsula. To break through into the Pacific, to see the mighty Cordilleras: that would be the climax of the whole voyage.

Aboard the *Beagle* and her sister ship, the *Adventure,* there was great commotion. A year's provisions were taken on board at Montevideo. On 7 December they waved goodbye (and good riddance) to the Rio Plata for the last time and headed south, out of the muddy estuary into the clear blue sea.

Pesos of Buenos Aires.

ABOVE The main Plaza of Buenos Aires, with the obelisk commemorating the independence of the city and known as the Altar of Liberty. BELOW Patagonian Indians. OVERLEAF General view of Buenos Aires from the Plaza de Toros.

CHAPTER VIII

THE ANDES

The Atlantic, now that they were about to leave it, made them a gift of some magical moments. One calm dry day a myriad butterflies came streaming past them far out at sea. It was like a snowstorm; as far as one could see, even with the aid of a telescope, the sky was filled with soft, white, fluttering wings, and it was not until the evening that a wind came up and blew them away.

Then one night they found themselves sailing along in a sea of gold: 'The vessel drove before her bows two billows of liquid phosphorus, and in her wake she was followed by a milky train. As far as the eye could reach the crest of every wave was bright . . .'

Christmas Day, 1833, found them far down the coast in the estuary of the Desire River, and it was the best Christmas they had in the whole five years' voyage. Darwin had shot a 170-lb guanaco on the day before, so there was fresh meat for every man. In the afternoon the crews of both ships came ashore for a contest of wrestling, jumping and running: 'Old men with long beards and young men without them were playing like so many children'. FitzRoy, in a benign mood, presented the prizes. It was all very different, Darwin remarks, from the usual Christmas celebration, every man getting as drunk as he could.

Physically Darwin was growing much stronger, stronger even than many of his shipmates, who were not able to climb mountains and stretch their legs on shore as he was. 'The greatest luxury', he wrote, 'is a shingle beach for a bed . . . I am quite astonished to find I can endure this life; if it was not for the strong and increasing pleasure from Natural History I never could'. But he was very tough. Witness the little incident that occurred one day when they were anchored at St Julian, a particularly arid stretch of the Patagonian coast; no trees, no bird or beast except for a sentinel guanaco. 'All was stillness and desolation. One reflected how many ages the plain had thus lasted, and how many more it was doomed

The halting-place of Villavicencio in the Andes, at sunrise.

Bivouac at the head of Port Desire inlet, Christmas 1833. Drawing by Conrad Martens.

thus to continue.' With FitzRoy and a party of men Darwin went ashore
to search for a freshwater source which was marked on an old Spanish
map. It was overwhelmingly hot, they were laden with instruments
and guns, and after some hours of tramping across the plain all except
Darwin were too exhausted to continue. However, from a hilltop they
could see what appeared to be some lakes about two miles distant, and
Darwin went off to explore. They watched anxiously while he stooped
down at the first lake and then immediately got up and went on to another,
where the same thing happened. Darwin walked slowly back with the
news that the water was salt.

They were now in a serious situation. FitzRoy and one of the sailors
were still quite unable to move and seemed to be getting worse. Darwin
did not much like leaving them with the vultures gathering ominously
round, but there was nothing for it but to return to the ship for help.
He set off on a forced march with the others, and by the time they had
reached the *Beagle* long after dark he had been on his feet continuously
for eleven hours without water. A rescue party brought back FitzRoy and
the sailor before morning.

Berkeley Sound, Falkland Islands, an 'undulating land, with a desolate and wretched aspect . . .'. [J]

Then they were away on their long sweep to the Falkland Islands, and, as we have seen, down to Tierra del Fuego for a last call on Jemmy Button. They passed through the Beagle Channel and Darwin recorded in his notebook: 'Channel about one and a half miles wide, hills on both sides above 2000 foot high . . . scenery very retired – many glaciers, uninhabited, beryl blue, *most beautiful*, contrasted with snow. Glacier: cliff to sea about 40 ft, blue by transmitted and reflected light. Channel covered by small icebergs – miniature arctic ocean'. They reached the Falkland Islands in March, and Darwin at once began to compare the insects and plants with those on the mainland. No detail escaped him. 'Saw a cormorant catch a fish and let it go 8 times successively like a Cat does a Mouse or otter a fish; and extreme wildness of shags.' A curious animal, the Falkland fox, lived there in great numbers, fearless enough to harass the men who went on shore. Darwin was confronted by a jackass penguin which brayed like an ass. He made a note that penguins use their wings as fins, some geese use theirs as paddles, and ostriches as sails.

There was one final delay before they entered the Pacific; the *Beagle* had bumped her bottom on a rock at Port Desire – some of her false keel had come away – and so they turned back to the mouth of the Rio Santa Cruz where she could be beached for repairs. All except her mainmasts were taken down, guns, anchors and other heavy gear were got ashore, and on the full tide they ran her up high and dry on the beach. Seeing that all their lives depended on her and she was their only hope of getting home, it was a little disturbing to see her like this, out of her element, perched up there with a sideways list on the sand. But the carpenters found little damage and were soon at work.

FitzRoy, with Darwin eagerly supporting him, had a plan to pass the time while the refit was going on. Except for a short distance inland the Rio Santa Cruz had never been explored. It was now decided that a party would go up the stream as far as it took them and perhaps get a glimpse of the Andes; better than that, they might even climb the mountains themselves. Three weeks' provisions were loaded into three boats, and they set off, twenty-five of them in all, with FitzRoy in command. At first the going was easy; they sailed upstream on the incoming tide, with a cloud of seabirds circling above them and sea-lions slithering down from the banks as they approached. On each side of the estuary and river lay arid plains of desert land; 'the general impression upon the mind is that of utter hopeless sterility'. Little rain and scarcely any drinking water; the guanacos drank the salt water of the *salinas*, and the pumas probably quenched their thirst in the blood of the guanacos. The river was much warmer than the air above, and at daybreak they noticed that it was smoking, as if it were boiling. Occasionally they came across ostriches swimming to get across the river.

Then the wind and the tide failed; ropes fitted with collars were passed ashore, and every man, FitzRoy included, took his turn at the heavy work of towing the boats upstream. It was a long way from being a joy-ride. By night it was bitterly cold, and sentries had to be posted in case of an Indian attack, and since FitzRoy felt bound to conserve his food supplies they were always hungry. Yet it was wonderfully refreshing to break into country where no civilised man had been before, or at any rate Darwin found it so.

Usually he went ahead with Bynoe to reconnoitre the way and to take potshots at any game that chanced to appear. A treeless plain of black lava spread away on either side, but here the guanaco swarmed – Darwin

ABOVE The *Beagle* laid ashore at the mouth of the river Santa Cruz. 'It was found that a piece of the false keel under the "fore-foot", had been knocked off, and that a few sheets of copper were a good deal rubbed.' [N] BELOW River Santa Cruz and distant view of the Andes. 'The curse of sterility is on the land, and the water flowing over a bed of pebbles, partakes of the same curse.' [J]

saw a herd of a thousand one day – and once again it was the survival of the fittest. For reasons of protection, no doubt, the guanacos slept in groups, with their tails to the centre, and changed their sleeping places each night. Darwin observed that they appeared to have favourite spots for lying down to die, and at one place the banks of the river were actually white with bones.

Let an animal go lame or perhaps fall ill and lag behind the rest, and

Hunting the guanacos. 'In many of their habits they are like sheep in a flock. Thus when they see men approaching in several directions on horseback, they become bewildered, and know not which way to turn.' ᴶ

the cat-like puma was upon it. Then from the foothills of the Andes, where they perched 'sultan-like' on the tops of the precipices, the condors would launch themselves into the air, marvellous fliers, hardly moving their wings. 'Except when rising from the ground, I do not recall having seen one of these birds flap their wings.' Directly the puma finished his meal, they came circling down to hack the carcass to pieces. These fierce birds attacked the young goats and lambs, and the shepherd dogs were trained to run out when they passed over and look upward, barking violently. One bird that Darwin shot had a wingspan of eight feet. There

146

ABOVE Cattle attacked by the condors. BELOW The two methods of hunting condors: baiting them with a carcass until they are trapped within an enclosure, and catching them with a rope and noose.

were two ways of trapping them: sometimes a carcass was left within an enclosure with a narrow entrance, and since the bird makes a running take-off along the ground once this entrance was closed they could not get away. They could be caught too in the trees where they roosted at night; a man would climb the tree and throw a noose round their neck – not so difficult as it sounds since condors are heavy sleepers. The birds were sold for 10s. apiece.

After ten days of toiling upstream the gleaming white crests of the Cordillera broke into view. But then they never seemed to get any nearer. Darwin yearned to reach them, and even went on ahead with FitzRoy on foot in an attempt to get to the foothills by a forced march. But it was no good. When they were 140 miles from the sea and the rations were running seriously low the mountains seemed just as distant as ever; in fact they were only 30 miles away, but it was too much. For FitzRoy it was not too disappointing—there they were, the mighty works of God, unchanged since eternity—but to Darwin it was maddening; how did the mountains get there? How long had they been there? What were the rocks of which they were composed? But there was no help for it; they had to turn back without an answer. In four days the three boats shot downstream with a current at 10 miles an hour to rejoin the *Beagle*. They found her 'afloat, fresh painted and as gay as a frigate'.

Now at last they set their course for the Pacific, and it would have been well at this stage if FitzRoy could have relaxed and taken things a little more easily. But they were tackling the icy straits of Tierra del Fuego in winter, and the weather was terrible. Great masses of ice frequently fell from the cliffs, and the crash reverberated like the broadside from a man-of-war through the lonely channels. 'The sight of such a coast', wrote Darwin, 'is enough to make a landsman dream for a week about shipwrecks, peril and death'. The rigging froze and the *Beagle's* decks were covered with snow.

It took them a full month to get through, and even then the Pacific did not greet them well; storms followed them all the way up to the coast of Chile. Rowlett, the purser, who was the oldest man on board (he was in his middle-thirties) had been ill for some time, and this rough and uncomfortable passage was more than he could stand. It was only a few months since Hellyer had been drowned in the Falkland Islands, and now in this close-knit little community it was a hateful thing to see another

ABOVE The Falkland fox *(Canis antarcticus)*. BELOW Argentinian oppossum *(Didelphis crassicaudata)*.

a   *b*

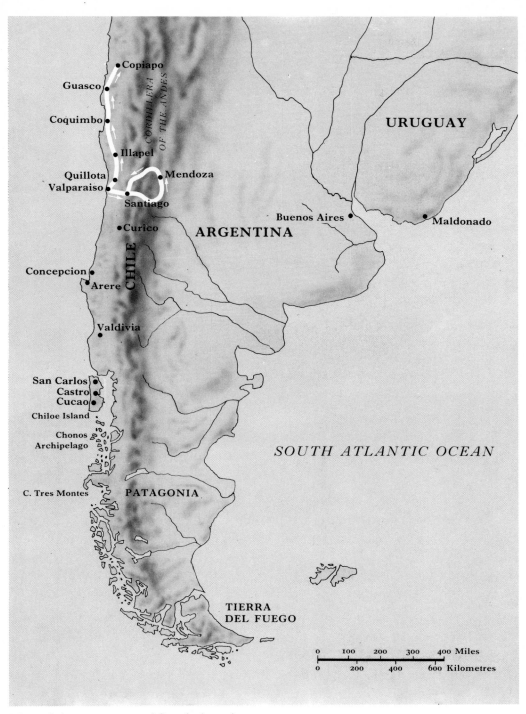

Map of the west coast of South America.

A bromelia found in the Andes *(Bromelia bicolor)*.

The port of Valparaiso.

shipmate go, to stand there bare-headed on the deck while FitzRoy read the service, and then lower the body with the Union Jack around it into the cold sea.

And so it was a gloomy and storm-battered little ship that arrived at last off Valparaiso (the Valley of Paradise) on 22 July 1834. But the sea was calm, the sun was shining at last, and after eight months out of touch with the world—eight months of monotonous food, of wet clothes and the perpetual heaving of the deck—it was an exhilarating thing for them to see a civilised town again, especially such a beautiful town as this. The white flat-topped houses straggled up the mountainside among trees and patches of green grass, and behind it rose up the tremendous backcloth

View of the Andes from the hills above Valparaiso Bay, with the peak of volcano Aconcagua on the right.

of the Andes. Good country smells came out from the shore, and the smoke from the homestead chimneys was a promise of fresh food and the sight of women once again. Letters from home were awaiting them, the third volume of Lyell's *Geology* had arrived, and even Darwin's walking shoes were in the packages from England. He lost no time in getting off the dank ship and taking up his quarters with Richard Corfield, an old schoolfellow he found living in the town. Then he was off on a mule to unravel the mystery of the Andes. He was away for six weeks.

There is something about Darwin's travels in the high Cordillera—and he made several trips there—that is especially sparkling and fresh. Of course he loved mountain climbing, but the Andes lifted up his spirits

Travelling in the Andes.

to the highest pitch, ideas crowded into his mind, one discovery led to another, and he was game for anything.

He stands on a crag high above Valparaiso, nothing around him but bare red rocks and the condors wheeling overhead, and the clarity of the air is such that Chile spreads out below as though it were a map. He can see the masts of the ships at anchor in the bay, 26 miles away. Behind him a 'fine chaos of mountains' spreads away. It is sublime, 'like hearing a chorus of the Messiah in full orchestra. I felt glad that I was alone'. In the teeth of a high wind coming in from the Pacific he sits his mule securely, and even on the most vertiginous passes and the most wobbly of suspension bridges he feels no giddiness. They are so high up that their potatoes boil but will not cook, and he must huddle up to his two guides for warmth at night, but the usual mountain sickness does not touch him.

There is so much to see: the alpine birds, especially the little tapaculo or 'cover up your posterior' bird that hopped about with its tail erect, and the turco, a ridiculous figure with its stilt-like legs popping from one bush to another with uncommon quickness; the puma which is driven up a tree and baited to death by the dogs, but utters no cry; the rat, very tame and abundant, that lives 'chiefly in hedges, curling its tail'. He saw what he thought was a cloud of heavy smoke, which turned out to be a swarm of locusts, flying north at a speed of some ten miles an hour. The great swarm, 2000 feet thick, came rushing on with a sound like wind going through the rigging of a ship, and Darwin joined the peasants in shouting and waving branches about in a vain effort to drive them away.

But it is the geology of the mountains that engrosses him, and he makes two discoveries that rivet his attention: at 12,000 feet he comes on a bed of fossil seashells, and then somewhat lower down a small forest of snow-white petrified pine trees with marine rock deposits round them. Now at last the 'marvellous story' was beginning to unfold. These trees had once stood on the shores of the Atlantic, now 700 miles away; they had been sunk beneath the sea, then raised 7000 feet. Clearly all this part of the South American peninsula was once submerged beneath the sea, and in quite recent geological times had been elevated again. As the Andes were pushed upwards they became at first a series of wooded islands and then a continuous chain of mountains whose cold climate killed off the vegetation as they rose. This movement had been accompanied by earthquakes and volcanic eruptions which acted like safety valves.

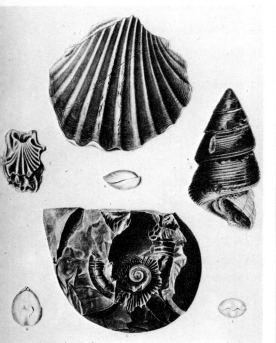 

LEFT Fossil sea-shells found on the Andes. RIGHT The tapaculo or 'cover up your posterior' bird (*Pteroptochos albicollis*). 'Well does the shameless little bird deserve its name, for it carries its tail more than erect.' ˡ

Not everyone was going to believe Darwin of course. Some of the Chileans wanted to know what he thought he was doing, roaming around in the mountains with his little hammer. 'It is not well', said a suspicious old Spanish lawyer. '*Hay un gato encenado aquí* (there is a cat shut up here). No country is so rich as to send out people to pick up such rubbish. I do not like it.' Darwin replied by asking him if he was not curious to know how the earthquakes and volcanoes occurred, why some springs were hot, others cold. These questions satisfied and silenced most people, but some, however, 'like a few in England who are a century behindhand, thought that all such enquiries were useless and impious; and that it was quite sufficient that God had thus made the mountains'. And FitzRoy? What was he, with his biblical notions, going to say to all this? Elated and excited by his discoveries Darwin set out for Valparaiso.

He got back to find that momentous things had been happening aboard the *Beagle* while he had been away, and that FitzRoy was in no condition to discuss this or anything else in a reasonable way; in fact, he had gone half out of his mind. What had happened was that a letter had arrived from the Admiralty in London flatly refusing to take on the expense of the extra ship; FitzRoy had acted without instructions, must pay all the costs himself, must dismiss the additional sailors he had enlisted, and must sell the ship at once. To any normal commander this would have been a severe rebuke; to FitzRoy it was an outrageous and unforgiveable blow at his pride. Perhaps he might have endured it had he been feeling well, but the strain of the last six months of danger and overwork showed clearly in his thin and worried face. He had been brooding on the many things that had gone wrong with the voyage; his scheme for christianising Tierra del Fuego, the death of Rowlett, the endless difficulties of the survey. Probably his arguments with Darwin had also upset him, and now this last blow was too much. The over-rigid self-control collapsed, hatred and rage took over, and he allowed his mind to go plummeting downward into complete despair. No doubt he thought of Captain Stokes, the previous captain of the *Beagle,* who had committed suicide in 1828, probably in the same cabin in which FitzRoy now passed so much of his time. He was going insane, he declared, there was nothing to be done; madness was in the family, his uncle Castlereagh had committed suicide and he was going the same way. He must resign; Wickham must take command and sail the ship directly to England.

It was in vain that Bynoe tried to calm him down, to reassure him that it was only from over-tiredness that he was suffering, that a little rest would put him right again. He was adamant; he was no longer fit to command.

This was the situation when Darwin got back to Valparaiso, and he thought it disastrous. He did allow himself for a moment to toy with the idea of going home, 'the exhaustless delight of anticipating the long wished-for day of return'. But to cut short his trip like this just when they had escaped from the accursed Tierra del Fuego into the Pacific—no, this was unthinkable. 'One whole night I tried to think over the pleasure of seeing Shrewsbury again, but the barren plains of Peru gained the day.' He would leave the *Beagle* and finish his investigations in the Andes; then a year or two later he would find his own way back to England.

It was Wickham who saved the day. He guessed correctly that what FitzRoy was really worrying about was his inability to complete the survey of Tierra del Fuego if he was left with only one ship. So now Wickham pointed out to FitzRoy that his instructions by no means obliged him to return to that dangerous coast; he was supposed only to give it as much time as he could spare before he embarked on his cruise through the Pacific. If he himself had command, Wickham went on, he had no intention of returning to Tierra del Fuego; he would carry out the original plan of returning to England on the much pleasanter Pacific route around the Cape of Good Hope. Thus there was every reason for FitzRoy to continue in command; he needed a respite on shore, and then he would feel much better when he got to sea again.

Little by little FitzRoy was pacified—no doubt he felt all the better for his outburst—and in the end he agreed to resume the command and to abandon the rest of the Fuegian survey. It was, incidentally, just as well that FitzRoy reached this decision, for the crew had had enough of Tierra del Fuego and a number of them were planning to desert if the *Beagle* returned there.

The *Adventure* was now sold for the surprisingly good price of £1400, and the *Beagle* made ready for sea again. Unfortunately FitzRoy felt the loss of the *Adventure* as a great blow: 'I confess', he said, 'that my own feelings and health were so much altered in consequence—so deprived of their former elasticity and soundness.' This may have been the cause of the next scene. Darwin had become quite badly ill on his return from the Andes; he thought from the effects of drinking coarse red wine, but it must have been something much more serious, perhaps the bite of the poisonous Benchuga bug, and although he was carefully nursed at Corfield's home, and was looked after by Bynoe (who prescribed calomel), it was over a month before he was on his feet again. FitzRoy delayed the departure of the *Beagle* for ten days on Darwin's account, and then paradoxically provoked a quarrel with him.

It was an absurd incident. FitzRoy remarked that since he and all the officers had been so generously entertained in Valparaiso he would have to give 'a great party to all the inhabitants of the place'. Darwin demurred; it was not really necessary, he thought. FitzRoy burst into a fury; yes, Darwin was just the sort of man who would take any favours and make no return. Darwin without a word got up and left the ship. When he returned a few days later FitzRoy, already on the road to recovery, behaved as though nothing had happened. Wickham, however, had had enough;

A family of Araucanian Indians. OVERLEAF Costumes of the Chilean rustics.

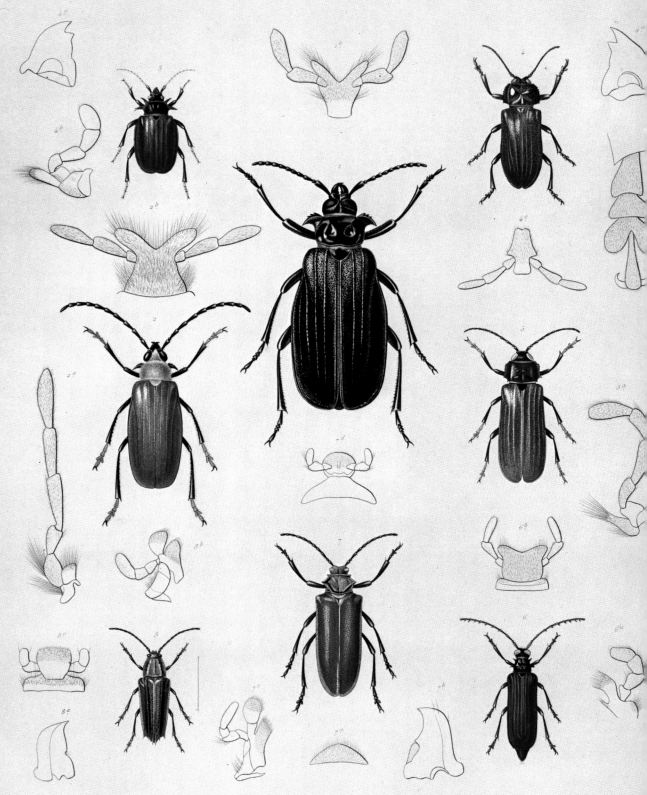

he drew Darwin aside and told him to stop making trouble with the captain. 'Confound you, philosopher, I wish you would not quarrel with the skipper; the day you left the ship I was dead tired and he kept me walking the deck till midnight abusing you all the time.'

One wonders a little where one is in all this. Was the mild Darwin getting more aggressive as the voyage went on? Had his hero-worshipping gone? Certainly he was not prepared now to accept FitzRoy's flat pronouncements about the truth of the Book of Genesis. In Valparaiso for the first time since the voyage began he had found a group of educated and intelligent men who were prepared to discuss scientific matters in an open-minded way, and it had been a great relief. FitzRoy could if he liked go on thinking that the Andes had never risen from beneath the sea, that the mountains had always been there and that the Flood had simply come up and covered them, but it was rubbish, he had positive proof that it was not so. There were other aspects about the Bible as well which were open to question. Wisely for the time being he kept these speculations to himself, but they were very much in his mind as they sailed south for their survey of the Chilean coast.

On 21 November they anchored in the bay of San Carlos, the capital of the island of Chiloe, and Darwin, as was his custom, immediately hired horses to investigate the country. He rode through green lush forests, over log roads, drenched by great rainstorms, and finally reached Castro, the ancient capital of Chiloe, 'a most forlorn and deserted place . . . the streets and plaza coated with fine green turf, on which sheep were browsing . . . not a watch nor a clock in the town; an old man struck the church bell by guess'. The people were of mixed blood, three-quarters Indian, and although they had plenty to eat they were miserably lacking in little luxuries; above all they longed for tobacco, and eagerly offered a fowl and a duck in exchange for a small twist. Darwin joined the *Beagle* again at San Pedro, and made an attempt with FitzRoy to climb to the summit of the island. But the forest was impenetrable. They were driven back by the sharp branches which tore at their face and hands, and the trailing bamboo creepers which enmeshed them like fishes in a net; the ground was covered with a mass of dead and dying trees, so that either they had to struggle along on hands and knees or clamber perilously along the tops of the tree trunks. Sometimes for ten minutes at a time their feet never touched ground, and they were so far off it—fifteen or twenty feet—that

A collection of coleoptera found in Chile.

The plaza of San Carlos de Chiloe.

the seamen jokingly called out the soundings. Finally they gave up in despair, and, much scratched and torn about, sailed away south.

There was one strange incident when they were beating up the wild and deserted coast near Cape Tres Montes. Bad weather drove them into a small harbour, and they were astonished to see what looked like a signal of distress from the land. A boat was sent ashore and brought back two seamen, members of a party of six who had deserted fifteen months before from an American whaler, and had since been wandering, helplessly lost, up and down the empty coast, coming across no trace of man or animal, except deer and nutria, in all that time. Almost the most remarkable feature was that they had kept a close reckoning of time and were only four days out. One of the men had been killed by falling off a cliff, but the *Beagle* rescued the other five, and they were found to be in better condition after a year of living on seal's flesh, shellfish and wild celery,

Old church at Castro, ancient capital of the island of Chiloe.

than any five sailors on board the *Beagle*. But as Darwin says, what a singular piece of good fortune they had in being thus rescued; had the *Beagle* not chanced to find them 'they might have wandered till they had grown old men, and at last have perished on this wild coast'.

With these men on board they ran back up the coast, anchoring here and there when harbours offered, and once came across a vast number of seals, which 'lay huddled together, fast asleep, like so many pigs; but even pigs would have been ashamed of their dirt, and of the foul smell which came from them'. The seals rose up and tumbled into the water and followed them back to the *Beagle*, expressing great wonder and curiosity. Then the ship met with a huge flight of petrels, hundreds of thousands of them flying by for hour after hour, blackening the sea when they settled and making a never-ceasing noise like a distant crowd.

At length after weeks of rough, tempestuous weather, quite out of

The crater of the volcano of Antuco at the beginning of an eruption.

touch with civilisation, they were back again at the island of Chiloe, and on 18 January 1835 they anchored for the second time in the bay of San Carlos. It was on this night that they saw the volcano Osorno, a hundred miles inland, in eruption. 'At 12 o'clock the sentry observed something like a large star, from which state it gradually increased in size till three o'clock, when most of the officers were on deck watching it. It was a very magnificent sight; by the aid of a glass, in the midst of the great red glare of light, dark objects in a constant succession might be seen to be thrown up and then fall down. The light was sufficient to cast on the water a long bright shadow. By the morning the volcano seemed to have regained its composure.' They were astonished to hear afterwards that the volcanoes of Aconcagua in Chile, 480 miles to the north, and Coseguina, 2700 miles north again, had also erupted that same night. All this was an overture for what was to come.

Ruins at Concepcion after the earthquake. Detail from a drawing by J. C. Wickham, first lieutenant on the *Beagle*.

CHAPTER IX

THE EARTHQUAKE

Four weeks later, almost to the day, the *Beagle* was anchored off the town of Valdivia, on the south Chilean coast, and on 20 February 1835 Darwin went ashore with Covington for one of his usual forays in search of new specimens. They wandered for a time through the apple orchards, and then lay down on the ground to rest. Suddenly a breeze swept through the trees and at the same time the ground began to tremble. Darwin and Covington started to their feet, and although they managed to stand up they felt very giddy and insecure. 'A bad earthquake', Darwin reflected afterwards, 'at once destroys the oldest associations; the world, the very emblem of all that is solid, had moved beneath our feet like a crust over a fluid; one second of time has created in the mind a strange idea of in-security, which hours of reflection would not have produced'. On board the *Beagle* it was as though the ship for a moment had slipped her anchors and was bumping on the bottom.

The real centre of the earthquake, however, was further to the north, and it was only when they sailed into the port of Talcahuano that they realised the full horror of what had happened. All the shore was strewn with debris, and it was 'as if a thousand great ships had been wrecked'. Burst bales of cotton, dead animals, uprooted trees, chairs, tables, even the roofs of houses lay tossed about on every side, and great masses of rock had fallen on to the beaches.

The people had been given little warning; at 10 a.m. large flights of seabirds were seen moving inland, and the dogs in the port took to the hills. But no one had thought much of these things at the time, and in any case at 11 o'clock the usual sea-breeze got up. Then at 11.40 a.m. the shocks began, and within a few seconds increased to an incredible violence. It was a curious twisting movement that made the ground rapidly open up into foot-wide fissures and then close again, and this was accompanied by a dry cracking sound. Meanwhile the sea was draining out of Talcahuano

Bay. A number of sailing ships were anchored there, three large whaling vessels, a barque, two brigs and a schooner, and all these were left keeling over in a wet plain of mud and soggy seaweed. The people ashore had by now bolted for high ground, expecting a great wave would follow, and thirty minutes after the first shock it came. With an appalling roar an enormous wall of water—a moving hill—rose up out of the sea and swept into the bay. In the ships the sailors took to the rigging and there they hung on for dear life as the wave went by and burst upon the town. Here it carried everything before it, loose timbers and bric-a-brac of every kind, whole houses with their furniture inside, even the horses, sheep and cattle that were grazing in the fields. All these were floated out to sea as the wave fell back and once again the ships in the bay were bumping on the bottom.

And now a second, larger wave came on and this too receded, only to be followed by a third that was greater still. The noise of the water was appalling. It was amazing the way most of the ships withstood this battering. They whirled around each other as if caught in a whirlpool, and although some of them collided their anchors held. The *Colocolo*, a Chilean naval schooner, was entering the bay at the time and safely rode the waves in deep water. So too did a number of smaller boats whose owners had managed to get out to sea before the waves had broken. Others were less lucky. A 30-foot schooner that was almost finished on the stocks was picked up and stranded in the middle of the ruins of the town. A nurse with a four-year-old English boy, the son of a naval captain, hoped to escape by jumping into a rowing boat, but the boat was dashed against an anchor and was split in half. The woman was drowned and it was hours later that the little boy was found drifting out at sea. Though wet and miserable he was sitting bolt upright on a piece of wreckage and still hanging on.

Out in the ocean the water turned black and seemed to be boiling; at two places columns of smoke were seen to be bursting up through the surface, and they had a loathsome sulphurous smell, the smell, so it seemed to the inhabitants, of hell itself. Large numbers of fish were poisoned. Then a whirlpool developed, and it appeared as if the floor of the sea had cracked open and that the sea was pouring itself into a vast cavity below. For some days afterwards high and low tides occurred several times an hour.

Inland the town of Concepcion was demolished in a matter of six

ABOVE The town of Talcahuano and port of Concepcion. BELOW Silver and copper works in the Andes.

TRARO

Caracara vulgaris.

seconds. Here too there was some little warning; women washing clothes in the river were startled to find that the water became muddy and rose with great rapidity from their ankles to their knees. The first shocks were not severe, and most of the people had just enough time to rush outdoors before the real cataclysm began—a mad thrashing about and bucketing of the earth that lasted for two minutes. Some clung to trees, others who threw themselves on to the ground were turned over and over like acrobats bouncing on a landing net. Poultry flew about screaming, horses stood trembling with their heads down and their legs stretched stiff and were thrown to the ground with their riders on top of them. It was impossible to see clearly what was happening because of the dust and smoke that filled the air, and in any case what was happening was unbelievable. The 6-foot-thick walls of the cathedral cracked and the roof fell in, whole streets of houses collapsed, and the people, running frenziedly through the dust and fires, kept calling to their families and friends who were buried under the heaving rubble. The heat was stifling, and each successive shock was preceded by a deep subterranean rumbling. These shocks continued with diminishing intensity at the rate of two or three an hour for the next week.

By the time the *Beagle* arrived at Talcahuano all was still, but a fearful stench of dead fish and animals and of decaying seaweed filled the air. FitzRoy and Darwin rode up to Concepcion to find that not a house was left standing; instead of streets there were merely lines of ruins. Many of the inhabitants were living in reed huts which had withstood the shock, and which the poor were now renting to the rich at excessive prices. Wickham executed a very competent sketch of the shattered cathedral.

This was no moment for petty triumphs, but as they walked about Darwin—no doubt with a gleam in his eye—was able to point out to FitzRoy that the level of the land was higher than it had been before, not much, just a few feet, but enough to prove that the earth *could* rise up out of the sea; and if a few feet, why not 10,000? Why not whole mountains? What other possible explanation was there for the fact that he had found beds of seashells high up in the Cordilleras?

This had been a bad earthquake, the worst that people could remember; it had run for 400 miles along the coast and it had been accompanied by the simultaneous eruption of a line of volcanoes. Could it not be, Darwin reasoned, that the centre of the earth was a raging furnace of

Carrion-feeding hawk *(Caracara vulgaris)*.

molten rock, and that from time to time this furnace burst through the earth's cold surface? Now finally he can say with confidence: 'We can scarcely avoid the conclusion, however fearful it may be, that a vast lake of melted matter of an area (here in Chile) nearly double the extent of the Black Sea is spread out beneath a mere crust of solid land . . . Nothing, not even the wind that blows, is so unstable as the level of the crust of the earth'. It was sobering to imagine this earthquake happening in England. What price then all the notions of empire and glory? All those great cities, the whole of British civilisation itself, could have vanished in an instant.

But neither Darwin nor FitzRoy was much disposed to argue at this moment. They were both shaken by what they had seen, and as they poked about among the ruins and talked to the survivors they learned many fascinating things not only about the earthquake itself but about human nature as well. Most of the people, like FitzRoy himself, believed that the disaster was caused by the will of God, probably as a punishment for human wickedness. Others spoke of an old Indian woman who was a witch; she had been offended when she had last passed through Concepcion and had taken her revenge by plugging up the vents of the volcanoes; and thus the earthquake had occurred. The number of dead, less than a hundred, would have been infinitely greater, Darwin learned, had not the people been accustomed to rushing out of doors directly they felt even the slightest shock, and the doors themselves they always kept open in case they jammed during an earthquake. But even this precarious way of living had not made them want to live elsewhere; they intended now to rebuild their houses exactly as they had been.

In Talcahuano thieves had been very active. Even while the earthquake was still going on and people were dying around them these monsters rooted about among the ruins, and paused only to cross themselves and to cry '*Misericordia*' whenever another shock occurred. In Concepcion, on the other hand, the disaster had been a mighty leveller of social distinctions; since rich and poor alike had lost everything they possessed they were disposed to be much kinder to one another. Now that it was all over, however, they were finding that the one thing they could not do without was money. Most of the town's currency had been destroyed. If Captain FitzRoy was going to sail up to Valparaiso for supplies would he kindly bring them them back as much money as he could?

The cathedral at Concepcion after the earthquake. Detail from a drawing by J. C. Wickham. 'The side which fronted the N.E. presented a grand pile of ruins, in the midst of which door-cases and masses of timber stood up, as if floating in a stream.'[1]

OVERLEAF The Uspallata range, north of Mendoza, 'separated from the main Cordillera by a long narrow plain or basin, like those so often mentioned in Chile, but higher, being six thousand feet above the sea . . . it consists of various kinds of submarine lava, alternating with volcanic sandstones and other remarkable sedimentary deposits'.[1]

Guanta, in the Coquimbo valley, at the foot of the Cordillera.

The earthquake had its effects on board the *Beagle* as well. It cleared the air. Where before there had been gloom and talk of resignations and desertions now everyone from the captain downwards began to count their blessings and feel more cheerful. Darwin was preoccupied with his geology. He stayed for a while with the hospitable Corfield when he got back to Valparaiso, and then in March 1835 set off again into the mountains. This was going to be a very rough journey indeed. He planned to cross the Cordilleras by the highest and most dangerous route, across the Portillo pass to Mendoza. He took with him two guides, ten mules and a *madrina*, a mare with a bell round her neck—a 'sort of stepmother to the whole group'. They rode for hour after hour in the icy wind, stopping only for Darwin to clamber up rocks, geological hammer in hand, fighting for breath at the high altitudes. On the ridges the atmosphere was so rarefied that even the mules were forced to stop every 50 yards; the Chileans recommended onions as a cure for the shortness of breath, but Darwin said that a good find of fossil shells was his best remedy. At night they

Muleteers at a camp fire.

slept on the bare earth. Yet the rewards were great: 'The peaks, already bright in the sun, appeared in gaps in the mist [to be] of stupendous height . . . cloudless, airy everlasting look'. The season was getting late; they met parties of men driving herds down from the higher valleys of the Cordilleras, and this sign of approaching winter hurried them on 'more than was convenient for geologising'. It is a proof of Darwin's extraordinary physical fitness at that time (so sadly to be denied him for the rest of his life) that when he got back from this trip, which took him twenty-four days, he said: 'Never did I more deeply enjoy an equal space of time'.

A couple of weeks later he was off again, this time along the coast road to Coquimbo and Copiapo, 500 miles away, where it was agreed that FitzRoy should pick him up in the *Beagle*. Once again he was worried about the money he was spending. It had cost him sixty pounds to cross the Andes and now he must draw a hundred pounds more. He wrote guiltily to his sister Susan: 'I verily believe I could spend money in the very moon'. Again he took guides, and bought horses and mules, but these he managed to sell again at the end of the journey for only two pounds less than he had paid. He got on well enough with his guides—the Chilean *guasos*—but he never liked them as much as his gauchos of the Pampas: 'The Gaucho may be a cut-throat but he is a gentleman; the guaso is an ordinary vulgar fellow'.

After a week of travelling along the coast road he got bored with the barren desert country and turned inland, up to the mining districts, where yellow pyrites were extracted under the most primitive and uneconomical conditions. Darwin, with his liberal principles, was appalled by the conditions in the mines; the workers, known as *apires,* or beasts of burden, were truly such. They carried loads of up to 200 lbs, for the greater part of the way climbing up notched poles placed in a zigzag line up the shaft. There was a rule that the miner was not allowed to halt for breath unless the mine was over 600 feet deep. These men carried on an average twelve loads a day, that is to say 2,400 lbs, from depths of 250 feet or more, and in addition to these gigantic efforts they were required to break up the ore when they had got it to the surface. Yet with all this Darwin was astounded to find them apparently healthy and cheerful. Their clothes were bizarre: long shirts of a dark coloured baize with a leather apron, fastened round the waist with a bright coloured sash, wide trousers and a close-fitting scarlet cap. He met a burial party one day; four men were carrying the corpse at a quick trot; after 200 yards they were relieved by four others who had dashed ahead on horseback. 'Thus they proceeded, encouraging each other by wild cries; altogether the scene formed a most strange funeral.'

By the beginning of June he was on his way down to Copiapo, travelling through country so sterile and arid that there was nothing at all for the horses to eat. One day they rode without stopping for twelve hours, but still found no possible fodder; the horses had had nothing for fifty-five hours and it was painful to listen to them gnawing at the hitching posts to which they were tied. In this part of the country rain only fell once in every two or three years, and the people depended entirely on snowstorms in the Andes above them; one good fall would give them water for a year. At last on 22 June Darwin reached Copiapo, and after one more short trip up into the mountains he joined up with the *Beagle* and they set off for Peru.

This time FitzRoy was not on board; he was off on an adventure of his own. While Darwin had been away in the Cordilleras the *Beagle* had been

Chilean miners, with their bright sashes and scarlet caps. 'Living for weeks together in the most desolate spots, when they descend to the villages on feast-days there is no excess or extravagance into which they do not run.' [J]

pushing ahead with her survey of the Chilean coast. Several events had conspired to rejuvenate FitzRoy. He was busy, and he always felt better when he was at sea. Then the Admiralty, in London, thinking no doubt that they had hit him a little too hard, decided to make a gesture. When the *Beagle* got back to Valparaiso from her second trip to Concepcion, FitzRoy got the news that he had been promoted; a message had arrived from London saying that he had been raised in rank from lieutenant to full captain. He of course showed no great elation; he merely complained that Wickham and Stokes had not been promoted too, but it was clear that nothing on earth could have pleased him more.

And now followed the bracing incident of the *Challenger*. She was a British man-of-war that had become a wreck in a storm at Arauco, south of Concepcion, and word had come through to Valparaiso that her commander, Captain Seymour, and his men were stranded in very wild country and having a rough time from the natives there. It was the business of HMS *Blonde*, the senior British man-of-war on the station, to go to the rescue, but her commander, an elderly commodore, showed much reluctance; he said he did not at all like getting on to a lee shore in the winter.

Now it happened that the stranded Captain Seymour was an old friend of FitzRoy's, and FitzRoy was not going to see him abandoned like this. He went aboard the *Blonde*, and argued hotly with the commodore, saying that it was all rubbish about the danger of the coast and that they must sail at once. And FitzRoy won the day; leaving Lieutenant Wickham to take the *Beagle* on to Copiapo he started off down the coast on the *Blonde* with himself as pilot. They anchored in the Bay of Concepcion, and he set out overland to find the *Challenger's* crew, nearly 100 miles away.

It was a hazardous trip and took some days; there was the problem of finding the right tracks, there were rivers with deceptive currents, there was little food, and the constant danger of an attack from the Indians. The horses grew tired, and FitzRoy was constantly obliged to sell the ones he had and buy fresh ones at exorbitant prices; often indeed their owners refused to part with them, since a fast horse was the only means of escape from an Indian attack. One day they met a party of Chileans who gave the alarming news that three thousand Indians had assembled and were expected to make an attack on the Chilean frontier; they had heard of the wreck and were actually on their way to plunder the crew when by accident they came up against a friendly tribe of Indians, who drove them back. FitzRoy hastened on. When finally he reached the shipwrecked crew he found that all but two were alive, but that many were sick and their provisions were low. They had built themselves a fortified encampment some miles from the wreck, but a plague of mice had fallen on the tents, and hundreds had to be killed every hour. The men were getting mutinous. FitzRoy and Captain Seymour talked far into the night, and at dawn next day FitzRoy set off back to the *Blonde* to get help. Finally the men were got back to Coquimbo, where a vessel was waiting to ship them back to England.

All this was very invigorating for FitzRoy. It was a little unfortunate perhaps that he should have felt it necessary to say to the reluctant commodore that he ought to be court-martialled, and the commodore had flown into a great rage; but FitzRoy seems not to have turned a hair. His duty done and his views clearly stated he returned in excellent spirits to the *Beagle*, which by then (August 1835) had arrived at Callao in Peru. 'The Captain', Darwin wrote home, 'is quite himself again'.

It was now nearly four years since they had left England, and they were all longing for home. Already three months earlier—eighteen months before he would in fact reach home—Darwin had written to Susan: 'I have not quite determined whether I will sleep at the Lion, the first night when I arrive per "Wonder", or disturb you in the dead of night; everything short of that is absolutely planned. Everything about Shrewsbury is growing in my mind bigger and more beautiful'. He chafed a little when FitzRoy went up to Lima to study some old charts and nautical papers which he thought might be of importance for the South American survey. FitzRoy to reassure him wrote a positively jaunty note: 'Growl not at all. Leeway will be made up. Good has been done unaccompanied by evil—ergo, I am happier than usual'. Darwin himself went up to Lima but found the country uninteresting, with the one exception mentioned before—'everything exceeded by ladies like mermaids'.

By this time he really had need of a spell of rest. He had driven himself very hard on his various journeys inland since the earthquake, sitting his mule from dawn to dark, cooking his meals by the campfire, sleeping on the ground in the open. His five hundred mile ride up from Valparaiso to Copiapo was not a jaunt that anyone else on the *Beagle* would have undertaken, and he himself admitted that, but for his interest in the

View of Lima from the sea near Callao.

geology of the country, it would have been 'downright martyrdom'. He had woken so often in the morning covered with flea bites that he regarded them as a natural condition. He had been bitten also by a more sinister insect than a flea: riding in the Cordilleras he mentions that one night he suffered an 'attack of the Benchuga'. The Benchuga bug is now thought to be the carrier of Chagas's disease, and these ill-omened bites might be one of the causes of the ill-health which was to bedevil Darwin for the rest of his life. He caught and kept one of the bugs, a soft black wingless insect about an inch long, and studied it for months. When placed on a table and presented with a finger, 'the bold insect would immediately protrude its sucker, make a charge . . . and draw blood'. The wound caused no pain, but in ten minutes the bug changed from being flat as a wafer to being round and bloated. One bite kept the bloodsucker fat for four months, but 'after the first fortnight it was quite ready to have another suck'.

Darwin was now satisfied that he had done all that was possible on the geology of the mountains. He turned his attention once more to that other larger question that was persistently at the back of his mind: the plants and the living creatures of the earth. Where had they come from? How had the different species been created? He had been able to gather some valuable new material on the way up the Chilean coast. There had been, for example, the fox he had seen on the island of Chiloe. The little animal had been so intent on watching the manoeuvres of the *Beagle* in the bay below that he had been able to walk up behind it and knock it on the head with his geological hammer. It proved to be a quite distinct and unknown species. Then there were the mice on the islands off the coast. How had they got there? Was it conceivable that owls or hawks might have caught live mice on the mainland and then have taken them to their young in their nests in the islands, and that some of these mice might have escaped to establish families there? There was also the problem of primitive man; he was still brooding on that.

At Callao ('a filthy, ill-built, small seaport', inhabited by a 'depraved, drunken set of people' in Darwin's opinion), he stayed on board while he was waiting for FitzRoy to return from Lima. He worked up his notes, packed his specimens (the fox was bound for the British Museum) and read books about the Pacific. 'Living quietly on board the ship and eating good dinners', he wrote to his sister Susan, 'have made me twice as fat and happy as I have been for some months previously'.

At last on 7 September 1835 they set sail, heading straight out into the open Pacific, where their first landfall was that strange little group of volcanic islands known as the Galapagos, or the Encantadas, the Enchanted Isles.

The Chilotan fox (*Canis fulvipes*), killed by Darwin with a knock on the head from his geological hammer.

Giant tortoises of the Galapagos (*Testudo nigra*). 'These huge reptiles, surrounded by the black lava, the leafless shrubs, and large cacti, seemed to my fancy like some antediluvian animals. The few dull-coloured birds cared no more for me than they did for the great tortoises.' [J]

CHAPTER X

THE GALAPAGOS ISLANDS

After Tahiti the Galapagos were the most famous of all the tropical islands in the Pacific. They had been discovered in 1535 by Fray Tomas de Berlanga, Bishop of Panama, and were now owned by Ecuador, 500 odd miles away. Already in the 1830s some sixty or seventy whalers, mostly American, called there every year for 'refreshments'. They replenished their water tanks from the springs, they captured tortoises for meat, (*galapagos* is the Spanish word for giant tortoises), and they called for mail at Post Office Bay where a box was set up on the beach. Every whaling captain took from it any letters which he thought he might be able to forward. Herman Melville called in at the Galapagos aboard the *Acushnet* not long after the *Beagle*'s visit, and the 'blighted Encantadas' are a part of the saga of the white whale. 'Little but reptile life is here found', wrote Melville, 'the chief sound of life is a hiss'.

Apart from their practical uses there was nothing much to recommend the Galapagos; they were not lush and beautiful islands like the Tahiti group, they were (and still are) far off the usual maritime routes, circled by capricious currents, and nobody lived in them then except for a handful of political prisoners who had been stranded there by the Ecuador government. The fame of the islands was founded upon one thing; they were infinitely strange, unlike any other islands in the world. No one who went there ever forgot them. For the *Beagle* this was just another port of call in a very long voyage, but for Darwin it was much more than that, for it was here, in the most unexpected way—just as a man might have a sudden inspiration while he is travelling in a car or a train—that he began to form a coherent view of the evolution of life on this planet. To put it into his own words: 'Here, both in space and time, we seem to be brought somewhat near to that great fact—that mystery of mysteries—the first appearance of new beings on this earth'.

For the *Beagle*'s crew, however, the islands at first were not earthly at all; they looked more like hell. The ship came up to Chatham Island, the most easterly of the group, in a fresh breeze and they saw a shore of hideous black lava that had been twisted and buckled and tossed about as though it were a petrified stormy sea. Hardly a green thing grew; the thin skeletal brushwood looked as if it had been blasted by lightning, and on the crumbling rocks repulsive lizards crawled about. Even the coconut palm, that emblem of the Pacific, was missing. A lowering sultry sky hung overhead and a forest of little volcanic cones that stuck up like chimney pots reminded Darwin of the iron foundries of his native Staffordshire. There was even a smell of burning. 'A shore fit for pandemonium', was FitzRoy's comment. 'The Infernal Regions . . .'

Yet they had good sport when the *Beagle* came to anchor in St Stephen's Harbour on 15 September 1835. Sharks, turtles and tropical fish popped up all around them, and it did not take the sailors long to get their lines over the side. 'This sport', Darwin noted, 'makes all hands very merry; loud laughter and the heavy flapping of fish (on the deck) are heard on every side'. There were several American whalers about, and one of them in particular, the *Science*, a big vessel carrying no less than nine whale boats, caught FitzRoy's expert eye. He thought her 'remarkably fine' as she came sailing majestically by.

A party landed on the black sand which was so hot that it burnt their feet through their thick boots. They found the shore littered with small barrows which the men from the whalers used to carry the huge tortoises down to the boats, and the great quantity of tortoise shells lying about were clear evidence of the massacres that went on. FitzRoy saw large terrapin shells used to cover young plants in a crude garden, instead of flower pots. Mr Stokes observed some tortoises which seemed to be enjoying themselves, 'snuffling and waddling about in the soft clayey soil near a spring'. Some of these were so large that when standing on their four elephantine legs they could reach the breast of a man with their heads. These tortoises weighed up to and over 500 lbs, and one that Darwin measured was 96 inches round the waist, and 53 inches down the length of its back. The peculiar lizards (actually they were iguanas) ran clumsily out of the men's way and shuffled into their burrows.

The *Beagle* cruised for just over a month in the Galapagos, and whenever they reached an interesting point FitzRoy dropped off a boatload of men to explore. On Narborough Island the turtles were coming in at night

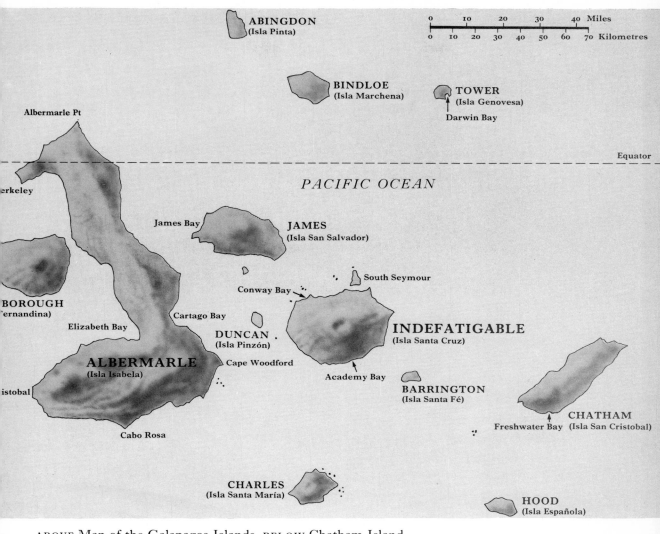

ABOVE Map of the Galapagos Islands. BELOW Chatham Island.

The marine iguana (*Amblyrhynchus cristatus*). 'It is a hideous-looking creature, of a dirty black colour, stupid and sluggish in its movements. The usual length of a full-grown one is about a yard, but there are some even four feet long.' [J]

to lay their eggs in the sand, thousands of them; they laid six eggs in each hole. On Charles Island there was a penal settlement of two hundred convicts, who cultivated sugar-cane, bananas and corn on the high ground. But the group that concerns us is the one that was put ashore on James Island. Here Darwin, Covington, Bynoe and two sailors were landed with a tent and provisions, and FitzRoy promised to come back and pick them up at the end of a week. Darwin visited other islands as well, but they did not differ very much from James Island, and so we can conveniently group all his experiences into this one extraordinary week. They set up their tent on the beach, laid out their bedding and their stores, and then began to look around them.

The marine lizards, on closer inspection, turned out to be miniature dragons, several feet in length, and they had great gaping mouths with pouches under them and long flat tails; 'imps of darkness', Darwin called them. They swarmed in thousands; everywhere Darwin went they scuttled away before him, and they were even blacker than the forbidding black rocks on which they lived. Everything about these iguanas was odd. They never went more than ten yards inland; either they sunned themselves on the shore or dived into the sea where at once they became expert swimmers, holding their webbed feet close to their sides and propelling themselves along with strong swift strokes of their tails. Through the clear water one could see them cruising close to the bottom, and they could stay submerged for a very long time; a sailor threw one into the sea with a heavy weight attached to it, and when he fished it up an hour later it was still alive and kicking. They fed on seaweed, a fact that Darwin and Bynoe ascertained when with Bynoe's surgical instruments they opened one up and examined the contents of its stomach. And yet, like some sailors, these marine beasts hated the sea. Darwin took one by the tail and hurled it into a big pool that had been left in the rocks by the ebb-tide. At once it swam back to the land. Again Darwin caught it and threw it back, and again it returned. No matter what he did the animal simply would not stay in the sea, and Darwin was forced to conclude that it feared the sharks there and instinctively, when threatened by anything, came ashore where it had no enemies. Their breeding season was November, when they put on their courting colours and surrounded themselves with their harems.

The other creatures on the coast were also strange in different ways; flightless cormorants, penguins and seals, both cold-sea creatures, unpredictably living here in these tropical waters, and a scarlet crab that scuttled over the lizards' backs, hunting for ticks. Walking inland with Covington, Darwin arrived among some scattered cactuses, and here two enormous tortoises were feeding. They were quite deaf and did not notice the two men until they had drawn level with their eyes. Then they hissed loudly and drew in their heads. These animals were so big and heavy that it was impossible to lift them or even turn them over on their sides— Darwin and Covington tried—and they could easily bear the weight of a man. Darwin got aboard and found it a very wobbly seat, but he in no way impeded the tortoise's progress; he calculated that it managed 60 yards in ten minutes, or 360 yards an hour, which would be roughly four miles a day—'allowing a little time for it to eat on the road'.

The tortoises were headed towards a freshwater spring on higher ground, and from many directions broad paths converged upon the spot. Darwin and Covington soon found themselves in the midst of a strange two-way procession, some of the animals going up, others coming down, all of them pacing deliberately along and occasionally pausing to browse on the cactus along the way. This procession continued all through the day and night, and appeared to have been going on for countless ages.

As they went higher the two men found themselves in quite different country; clouds filled the air with moisture and there were tall trees covered with ferns, orchids, lichens and mosses. At the spring itself one line of tortoises were quietly leaving, having drunk their fill, and another line were eagerly travelling towards the water, with outstretched necks. 'Quite regardless of any spectator, the tortoise buries his head in the water above his eyes, and greedily swallows great mouthfuls, at the rate of about ten in a minute.' They drank and drank as though they were not drinking for one day but for a month, as indeed they were.

The males were easily distinguished from the females by their greater size and their longer tails; during the mating season the male utters a hoarse bellow which can be heard a hundred yards away. 'The female', says Darwin briskly, 'never uses her voice'.

The huge beasts were quite defenceless. Whalers were taking them by the hundred to provision their ships, and Darwin himself had no difficulty in catching three young ones which were later put on board the *Beagle* and taken back alive to England. Natural hazards beset them too, of

Sailor with a boat-hook for turning over tortoises.

course; the carrion-feeding buzzards swooped on the young tortoises as soon as they were hatched, and occasionally Darwin would come upon the body of some monster who in his old age had missed his footing and fallen down a precipice. Everywhere through the islands discarded shells lay about. Roast tortoise, Darwin discovered, was good eating, especially if you cooked it as he had seen the gauchos cook the armadillos—in the shell.

Another phenomenon was the land iguana. These were almost as big as the marine iguana—a 4-foot specimen was nothing unusual—and even

The land iguana (*Amblyrhynchus demarlii*). 'Like their brothers of the sea-kind, they are ugly animals, of a yellowish orange beneath and of a brownish red colour above . . . When not frightened, they slowly crawl along with their tails and bellies dragging on the ground. They often stop and doze for a minute or two, with closed eyes and hind legs spread out on the parched soil.' [J]

uglier; they had a ridge of spines along the back and a Joseph's coat of orange-yellow and brick-red that looked as though it had been splashed upon them in blotches by a clumsy hand. They fed upon the 30-foot cactus trees, climbing up quite high to get at the more succulent bits, and always seemed to be ravenous; when Darwin threw a group of them a branch one day they fell upon it, pulling and tugging it away from one another like dogs quarrelling over a bone. Their burrows were so numerous that Darwin was constantly putting his foot into them as he walked along, and they could shift the earth with astonishing rapidity, one quick scrape with the front paws and then another with the back. They had sharp teeth and

The Galapagos hawk *(Craxirex galapagoensis)* by John Gould.

a general air that was menacing, yet they never seemed to want to bite. 'Essentially mild and torpid monsters', they crawled slowly along, tails and bellies dragging on the ground, and often stopped for a short doze. Once Darwin waited until one of them had got himself fairly underground and then pulled him by the tail. Surprised rather than angry the animal whipped round and eyed Darwin indignantly as if it were saying, 'What did you pull my tail for?' But it did not attack. Its meat when cooked was white and not too bad, not at any rate as Darwin says 'for those whose stomachs soar above all prejudices'.

On James Island Darwin counted twenty-six species of land birds, all unique. 'I paid also much attention to the Birds', he wrote to Henslow, 'which I suspect are very curious'. They were incredibly tame. Having never learned to fear man they regarded Darwin simply as another large harmless animal, and they sat unmoved in the bushes whenever he passed by. He brushed a hawk off a bough with the end of his gun. A mocking-bird came down to drink from a pitcher of water he was holding in his hand, and at the pools in the rocks he knocked off with a stick or even with his hat as many doves and finches as he wanted. He quotes a paradisial description from Cowley, written in the year 1684: 'Turtle-doves were so tame that they would often alight upon our hats and arms . . . they not fearing man'. Alas that Cowley goes on to say that 'such time as some of our company did fire at them . . . they were rendered more shy'. In the same year Dampier remarked that a man in a morning's walk might kill six or seven dozen of these doves. On Charles Island Darwin saw a boy sitting by a well with a switch in his hand, with which he killed the doves and finches as they came in to drink; the boy told him that he was in the habit of getting his dinner this simple way. The birds never seemed to realise their danger. 'We may infer', wrote Darwin, 'what havoc the introduction of any new beast of prey must cause in a country, before the instincts of the indigenous inhabitants have become adapted to the stranger's craft or power'.

But still at that time most of the inhabitants of the Galapagos islands lived in peace together. Darwin saw a finch unconcernedly eating one end of a bit of cactus while a lizard ate the other, and in the upper, greener regions lizards and tortoises fed together on the same bush of berries.

And so an enchanted week went by, and Darwin's jars were filled with plants, seashells, insects, lizards and snakes. The Garden of Eden pre-

196   The Galapagos turtle-dove (*Zenaida galapagoensis*), by John Gould. OVERLEAF *Midshipman's Berth*, by Augustus Earle.

Zenaida Galapagoensis.

sumably was not quite like this, nevertheless the island had a quality of timelessness and innocence, nature was in a state of balance with itself, and the only real intruder here was man. One day they walked around the coast to a crater which contained a perfectly circular lake. The water was only a few inches deep, and it rested on a floor of sparkling white salt. The shore was covered with a fringe of bright green plants. In this idyllic spot the mutinous crew of a whaling ship had murdered their captain a short time before, and the dead man's skull was still lying on the ground.

The whalers, however, were not all as ferocious as this, and indeed Darwin and Bynoe were very grateful when an American vessel visited the island and provided them with three casks of water which they needed badly, and a welcome bucket of onions. 'Extraordinary kindness of Yankeys', Darwin noted in his diary.

But the *Beagle* could not linger, much as Darwin longed to. 'It is the fate of most voyagers, no sooner to discover what is most interest in any locality, than they are hurried from it.' Back on board he began to sort out his specimens, and was soon struck by an important fact: the majority of them were unique species which were to be found in these islands and nowhere else, and this applied to the plants as well as to the reptiles, birds, fish, shells and insects. It was true that they resembled other species in South America, but at the same time they were very different. 'It was most striking', Darwin wrote later, 'to be surrounded by new birds, new reptiles, new shells, new insects, new plants, and yet by innumerable trifling details of structure, and even by the tones of voice and plumage of the birds, to have the temperate plains of . . . Patagonia, or the hot dry deserts of northern Chile, vividly brought before my eyes'.

He made another discovery: the species differed from island to island, even though many of the islands were only fifty or sixty miles apart. His attention was first drawn to this by comparing the mocking-thrushes shot on various islands, but then Mr Lawson, an Englishman who was acting as vice-governor of the archipelago, remarked that he could tell by one look at a tortoise which island it came from. Thus the tortoises of Albemarle Island had a different sort of shell from those on Chatham, and both differed again from those on James.

With the little finches these effects were still more marked. The finches were dull to look at, and made dreary unmusical sounds; all had short tails, built nests with roofs, and laid white eggs spotted with pink, four to a

The cactus-feeding finches (*Cactornis scandens*), by John Gould.   201 clutch. Their plumage varied within limits: it ranged from lava black to green, according to their habitat. (It was not only the finches that were so dully feathered; with the exception of a yellow-breasted wren and a scarlet-tufted flycatcher none of the birds had the usual gaudy colouring of the tropics.) But it was the number of different species of finch, and the variety of their beaks, that so amazed Darwin. On one island they had developed strong thick beaks for cracking nuts and seeds, on another the beak was smaller to enable the bird to catch insects, on another again the beak was adjusted to feeding on fruits and flowers. There was even a bird that had learned how to use a cactus spine to probe grubs out of holes.

Clearly the birds had found different foods available on different islands, and through successive generations had adjusted themselves accordingly. The fact that they differed so much among themselves as compared with other birds suggested that they had got to the Galapagos islands first; for a period, possibly quite a long one, they were probably without competitors for food and territory, and this had allowed them to evolve in directions which would otherwise have been closed to them. For instance, finches do not normally evolve into woodpecker-like types because there are already efficient woodpeckers at work, and had a small mainland woodpecker already been established in the Galapagos it is most unlikely that the woodpecker finch would ever have evolved. Similarly the finch which ate nuts, the finch which ate insects, and the finch which fed on fruit and flowers, had been left in peace to evolve their best method of approach. Isolation had encouraged the origin of new species.

Somewhere here a great principle was involved. Naturally Darwin did not grasp the full implications of it all at once; for instance, he makes little mention of the finches in the first published edition of his Journal, yet the subject of their diversity and modification later became one of the great arguments in his theory of natural selection. But by this time he must have realised that he was on the edge of a remarkable and disturbing discovery. Until this point he had never openly objected to the current belief in the creation of unchangeable species, though he may well have had secret doubts. But now here on the Galapagos, faced with the existence of different forms of mocking-birds, tortoises and finches on different islands, different forms of the same species, he was forced to question the most fundamental contemporary theories. Indeed, it was more than that; if the ideas that were now buzzing round in his head were proved correct then

ABOVE An example of large-beaked finches (*Geospiza strenua*). BELOW Comparative sizes of the beaks of four species of Galapagos finches.

203

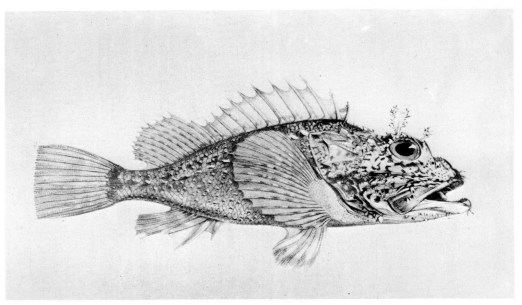

Two fishes of the Galapagos. ABOVE *Scorpoena histrio*. BELOW *Tetrodon angusticeps*.

all the accepted theories of the origin of life on this earth would have to be revised, and the Book of Genesis itself – the story of Adam and Eve and the Flood – would be exposed as nothing more than a superstitious myth. It might take years of research and investigation to prove anything, but in theory at least all the pieces of the jig-saw seemed to be coming together.

He can hardly have failed to have put his ideas to FitzRoy if only in a tentative, speculative way; and if we follow the two men's later writings it is not impossible to reproduce their argument, not impossible to envisage them here in their narrow cabin, or, if you like, out on the poop deck on a calm night as they sailed away from the Galapagos, putting forth their ideas with all the force of young men who passionately want to persuade one another and to get to the absolute truth.

Darwin's thesis was simply this: the world as we know it was not just 'created' in a single instant of time; it had evolved from something infinitely primitive and it was changing still. There was a wonderful illustration of what had happened here in these islands. Quite recently they had been pushed up out of the sea by a volcanic eruption such as they had seen in Chile, and at first there was no life at all upon them. Then birds arrived, and they deposited seeds from their droppings, possibly even from mud clinging to their feet. Other seeds which were resistant to sea-water floated across from the South American mainland. Floating logs may have transported the first lizards across. The tortoises may have come from the sea itself and have developed into land animals. And each species as it arrived adjusted itself to the food – the plant and animal life – that it found in the islands. Those that failed to do so, and those that could not defend themselves from other species, became extinct. That is what had happened to the huge creatures whose bones they had discovered in Patagonia; they had been set upon by enemies and destroyed. All living things had been submitted to this process. Man himself had survived and triumphed because he was more skilful and aggressive than his competitors, even though in the beginning he was a very primitive creature, more primitive than the Fuegians, more primitive even than the apes. Indeed, it was possible that all forms of life on earth had started from one common ancestor.

FitzRoy must have thought that all this was blasphemous rubbish, since it was in flat contradiction to the Bible; man, it was definitely stated there, was created perfect, the image of God Himself, and all the different

species, plants as well as animals, were created separately and had not changed. Some had simply died out, that was all. He even went so far as to turn the question of the finches' beaks to support his own theories: 'This appears to be one of those admirable provisions of Infinite Wisdom by which each created thing is adapted to the place for which it was intended'.

FitzRoy as the voyage progressed had become more and more rigid in his biblical views. He believed that there were some things that we were not meant to understand; the explanation of the original source of the universe must remain a mystery which defied all scientific investigations. But by now Darwin had gone too far to be able to accept this; he could not stop short at the Bible, he had to go beyond it. Civilised man was bound to go on asking that most vital of all questions, 'Where have I come from?', and to follow his enquiries wherever they took him. Perhaps they would lead him nearer to God than any act of blind faith could ever do.

There was to be no end to this argument. It was, in fact, an anticipation of that clash of opposite opinions, the one scientific and exploratory and the other religious and conservative, that was to take place at the bitter meeting in Oxford twenty-five years later. For the moment, however, the two men could do no more than agree to disagree; Darwin certainly did not push his ideas too hard, and there still remained a great deal of personal liking between the two young men. The future was to carry them far apart, but just now they were together and still dependent on one another. The voyage itself conspired to put aside their differences.

Species of Doris, found in the Southern Pacific.

1 5 Doris violacée (NOUV. HOLLANDE)   8 11 Doris galonnée (ILE-DE-FRANCE)

4 7 Doris orangée (NOUV. HOLLANDE)   12 13 Doris sale   (ILE-DE-FRANCE)

14 17 Doris enfumée (ILE-DE-FRANCE)

HOMEWARD BOUND

The *Beagle* now was a happy ship. She was homeward bound. In the swell of the tropical Pacific she bowled along at the rate of 150 miles a day. With great good luck just before she sailed from the Galapagos she had fallen in with a little schooner from Guayaquil, and there had been a bag of mail for them aboard the vessel. They had fresh meat; eighteen live turtles were lying on their backs on the after deck. FitzRoy spent his time writing up his account of the voyage. 'The Captain is daily becoming a happier man; he now looks forward with cheerfulness to the work which is before him.' Darwin was busy in his cabin, that had now become a miniature laboratory, almost, you might say, a little natural history museum; every cranny was stuffed with snakes and insects in jars, the skins of birds and other creatures, and he sat at his table, pretty much as he was to sit for the rest of his life, with his microscope, his dissecting instruments and his notebooks before him.

Darwin, now nearly twenty-six, had changed in appearance since they had left Plymouth four years before; he had filled out, his head had become a little heavier, and in his manner there was more assurance and authority. His studies now possessed him absolutely. 'I literally could hardly sleep at night for thinking over my day's work', he had written to Susan. He did not even bother to shoot or fish for specimens any more – all that was left to Covington. Also he had grown shabbier. One by one the elegant waistcoats and fine white shirts that he had brought aboard had been mended, patched and finally discarded. He was now rigged out more as a sailor.

The bulk of the *Beagle*'s work was done – she had merely to complete her chain of chronological reckonings round the world – and so there was a less purposeful atmosphere on board, the relaxed air of a cruise rather than a scientific voyage, and it was a matter of long uneventful weeks at sea punctuated by pleasant landfalls at Tahiti, New Zealand and Australia.

A Maori chief, wearing the feather-trimmed cape of his rank.

Matavai Bay, Tahiti, where the *Endeavour* had anchored in 1769.

It took them twenty-five days, running before the steady trade-wind, to cover the 3200 miles from the Galapagos to Tahiti, and on 15 November 1835 they anchored, as Captain Cook had done sixty-six years before them, in Matavai Bay. Immediately they were surrounded by dozens of canoes, and when they landed at Port Venus (again, what memories of Cook) they were greeted by a crowd of happy, laughing men, women and children. 'Charming Tahiti!' exclaimed Darwin. He was delighted with it all. He found the island beautiful and the inhabitants hospitable: 'There is a mildness in the expression of their countenances which at once banishes the idea of a savage'. But rather surprisingly he was disappointed by the

212

Both Darwin and FitzRoy were disappointed in the appearance of the women of Tahiti, and Darwin thought they were in great need of a becoming costume.

women: 'Their personal appearance . . . is far inferior in every respect to that of the men . . . . Most of the men are tattooed . . . so gracefully that they have a very elegant effect. One common pattern is somewhat like the crown of a palm-tree. It springs from the central line of the back, and gracefully curls round both sides. The simile may be a fanciful one, but I thought the body of a man thus ornamented was like the trunk of a noble tree embraced by a delicate creeper. Many of the elder people had their feet covered with small figures so placed as to resemble a sock . . . The women are tattooed in the same manner as the men, and very commonly on their fingers'.

The breadfruit *(Artocarpus altilis)* 'conspicuous from its large, glossy and deeply digitated leaf'.[J]

At daybreak next morning, even before the *Beagle*'s crew had had time to have breakfast, the ship was hemmed in by canoes, and at least two hundred natives eagerly swarmed on board. Every one of them had brought something to sell, mostly shells, but by now they were well aware of the value of money and were no longer interested in nails, or old clothes. Most of the men knew a few English words, so that 'a lame sort of conversation could be carried on'. One of the Tahitians to whom Darwin had given some trifling gift brought him a present of hot roasted bananas, a pineapple and some coconuts, and Darwin was so pleased with this 'adroit attention' that he engaged the man and a companion to accompany him as guides on a three-day trip into the mountains.

It would be hard to imagine anything less like his perilous and carefully-planned excursions into the mountains in South America. Darwin had told his two guides to bring food and clothing with them, but they replied that there was plenty of food in the mountains, and for clothing their skin was sufficient. And indeed they lived off the land with the greatest ease and comfort. When they stopped for the night the two Tahitians in a few minutes built an excellent hut of bamboos thatched with banana leaves; they dived into a pool and 'like otters, with eyes open followed the fish into holes and corners and thus caught them'. They cooked delicious meals of fish and bananas wrapped up in small green parcels of leaves which they roasted between two layers of hot stones, and which they themselves enjoyed with uninhibited pleasure. 'I never saw any men eat near so much.'

Darwin had been told that the Tahitians had become a gloomy race, living in fear of the missionaries, but this he found to be decidedly untrue. 'It would be difficult in Europe', he wrote, 'to pick out of a crowd half so many merry and happy faces'. Yet there was one revealing little incident. Up in the mountains he offered his guides a drink from his flask of spirits; 'they could not resolve to refuse; but as often as they drank a little, they put their fingers before their mouths and uttered the word "Missionary"'. A sort of incantation, one imagines, to soothe their consciences.

On Sunday FitzRoy led a party to divine service in the chapel in Papeete, the capital of the island; Mr Pritchard, the leading missionary in the island, performed the service, first in Tahitian, then in English, and the chapel was filled with 'clean, tidy people'. Afterwards they returned on foot to Matavai, through groves of bananas, coconuts, oranges and the glossy breadfruit tree.

ABOVE View of Tahiti near Matavai, by Conrad Martens. BELOW Interior of a Tahitian
hut. 'Upon slight posts, placed in the ground in a long ellipse, a very light and elegant
framework of "purau" is supported. This framework forms the low, but extensive roof,
and upon it a thatch of pandanus leaves . . .' [N]

Queen Pomare of Tahiti, 'a large awkward woman without any beauty, grace or dignity. She has only one royal attribute – a perfect immovability of expression under all circumstances, and that a rather sullen one'. [1]

One of FitzRoy's missions on Tahiti was to demand compensation from the reigning queen, Pomare, for a small English vessel which the Tahitians had plundered some two years earlier; a sum in recompense had been agreed upon but no money had been forthcoming. A parliament was held, and all the chiefs assembled. 'I cannot sufficiently express our general surprise', wrote Darwin, 'at the extreme good sense, the reasoning powers, moderation, candour, and prompt resolution, which were displayed on all sides . . . . The chiefs and people resolved to complete the sum which was wanting . . . and a book was opened early next morning, making a perfect conclusion to this very remarkable scene of loyalty and good feeling'. After the discussion was ended, several of the chiefs gathered round and questioned FitzRoy on international customs and laws relating to ships and foreigners, and the meeting ended with FitzRoy inviting Queen Pomare to visit the *Beagle* that night. He had already had an audience with her, and found her living in a cottage in great simplicity and very little style, attended by only a few ill-dressed 'maidens'. The ceremony merely consisted in shaking hands, and FitzRoy found her sad and unprepossessing, 'a large awkward woman'. Nonetheless, when she came on board the *Beagle* she was received with great ceremony; four boats were sent to meet her, the ship was dressed, the yards were manned, and the sailors gave her three cheers as she came on board. After dinner FitzRoy put on a show of fireworks and the sailors sang hymns. At one moment they burst into a comic, rather bawdy song, but the interpreter hastily explained it as 'sea-singing'. The queen received all these attentions with 'a perfect immovability of expression', but she stayed on board till after midnight.

Next day, 26 November, the *Beagle* set sail and steered a course for New Zealand. They were at sea for more than three weeks. 'It is necessary to sail over this great ocean to comprehend its immensity', wrote Darwin; '. . . for weeks together . . . nothing but the same blue, profoundly deep ocean . . . The meridian of the Antipodes has likewise been passed . . . calling to mind old recollections of childish doubt and wonder. Only the other day I looked forward to this airy barrier as a definite point in our voyage homewards, but now I find it, and all such resting-places for the imagination, are like shadows, which a man moving onwards cannot catch'. It was 21 December 1835 when they sailed into the Bay of Islands, up in the north-west corner of the North Island.

Monument to the daughter of a Maori chief. OVERLEAF *Tahiti, revisited*, by William Hodges.

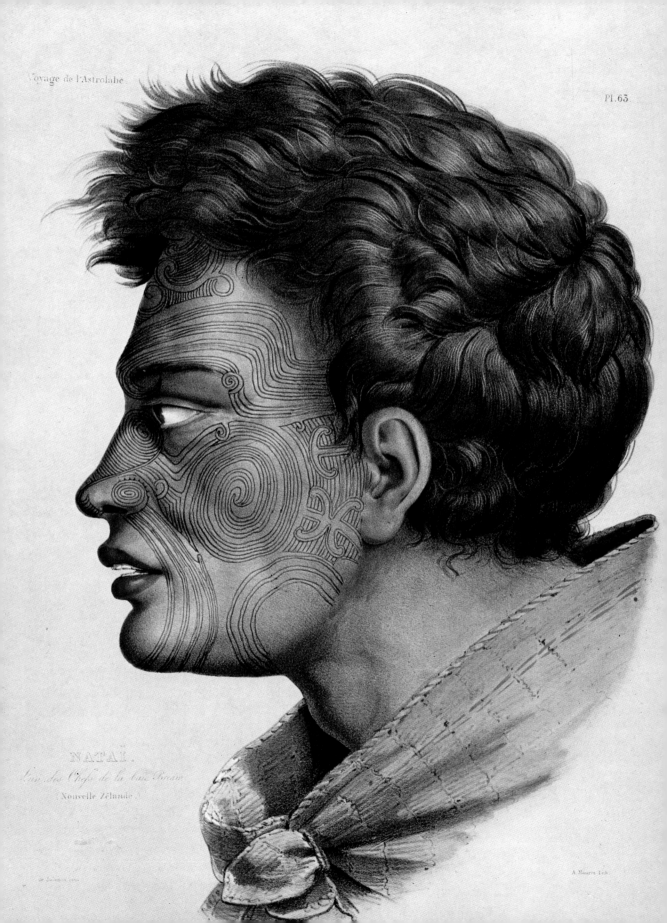

Pl.65

NATAÏ.
Un des Chefs de la baie Bream
(Nouvelle Zélande)

A. Maurin Lith.

The first sight of the place was not impressive. Little villages of square, tidy-looking houses came down to the water's edge; they belonged to the English settlers who had tried to re-create English cottage gardens of roses, honeysuckle and sweet-briar in this alien soil. Darwin felt a sharp pang of homesickness for real English gardens. There were three whalers at anchor in the bay, but there was an air of dullness and inactivity; only one canoe came alongside the *Beagle* – 'a not very pleasing contrast with our joyful and boisterous welcome at Tahiti'. When they got on shore they found the contrast even more displeasing. The native New Zealanders compared badly in every way with the Tahitians; Darwin even goes so far as to say 'one is a savage, the other a civilised man'. They were extremely dirty and the idea of washing never seemed to enter their heads; most of them were dressed in a couple of blankets, black with dirt, and their faces were entirely covered by a complicated design of tattooing which gave them a disagreeable expression. They were surly and inhospitable. Only one thing about them took Darwin's fancy; their habit of rubbing noses when they met. The rubbing lasted rather longer than a cordial shake of the hand, and was accompanied by 'comfortable little grunts'. He was interested to note the strange lack of ceremony between master and slave; although the chief had power of life and death over him, the slave would rub noses with anyone he met, either before or after his master, regardless of any rules of precedence.

The one bright spot for Darwin in his stay in New Zealand was his visit to Waimate, a settlement which the missionaries had made about fifteen miles from the Bay of Islands. He went there first by boat and then on foot, walking through desolate, uninhabited country, overgrown with fern, and was overjoyed when he arrived at the English farmhouse, with its well-tilled crops, farm animals, even a mill, the whole 'placed there as if by an enchanter's hand'. His nostalgia for England grew even stronger, particularly when he watched the mission natives playing a game of cricket. The cleanliness and healthy appearance of these natives struck him the more forcibly by contrast with the spectacle he had seen when he visited a village where the daughter of a chief, a heathen, had recently died. She was placed upright between two canoes and put inside an enclosure painted bright red and ornamented with wooden images of the native gods. Her relations were gathered round the enclosure, howling and tearing at their flesh – 'filthy, disgusting objects'.

Head of a New Zealander with tattooes.

Head of a New Zealander. 'The lines upon the face are not . . . arbitrary marks, invented or increased at the caprice of individuals, or the fancy of the operator who inflicts the torture; they are heraldic ornaments, distinctions far more intelligible to the natives of New Zealand than our own armorial bearings are to many of us . . .' [N]

ABOVE The ceremony of *ongi* or rubbing noses. 'My companion standing over them, one after another, placed the bridge of his nose at right angles to theirs and commenced pressing. This lasted rather longer than a cordial shake of the hand with us; and as we vary the force of the grasp, so do they in pressing.' ¹ BELOW Lamentation over the body of a chief.

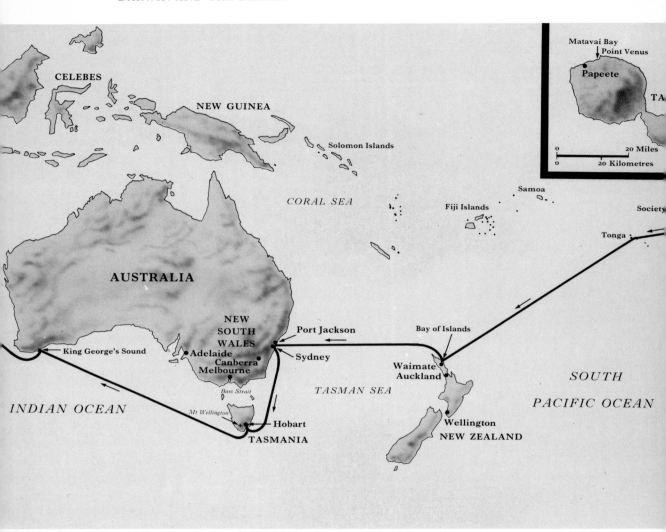

Map of the Pacific and Australasia.

One native custom was too deeply rooted for the missionaries to suppress, even on their settlement: the universal habit of tattooing. When a famous tattooist from the south island arrived at the farm the wives of the missionaries tried to persuade the dairymaids not to be tattooed, but they said, 'We really must just have a few lines on our lips; else when we grow old . . . we shall be so very ugly'.

His experiences with the missionaries here, and with the ones he had met in Tahiti, aroused an interest which remained with Darwin to the

Missionary settlement near the Bay of Islands.

end of his life, and this was one point he had in common with FitzRoy, himself a fanatical proselytiser. While still at sea in the following year they wrote a pamphlet with their joint signatures pressing for more Government support for the missionaries in the Pacific; it was finished by the time they touched in at Cape Town, and was published in the *South African Christian Recorder* in September 1836, one of Darwin's earliest signed publications.

During his short stay in New Zealand Darwin learned of the one-time existence of the giant prehistoric bird, the Moa (*Dinornis robustus*). Little was known about this terrifying creature, which stood 10 to 12 foot high, but it was thought to have become extinct in comparatively recent times. It was one of those strange anomalies in nature, a flightless bird; remembering the flightless cormorants in the Galapagos Darwin concluded later that the use of wings could be a disadvantage in the case of birds and insects living on oceanic islands, where a sudden storm might catch their wings and blow them out to sea.

Nine days in New Zealand were enough, and on 30 December the *Beagle* set off for Australia. 'I believe we were all glad to leave New Zealand', Darwin noted in his journal. 'It is not a pleasant place. Among the natives there is absent that charming simplicity which is found at Tahiti, and the greater part of the English are the very refuse of society.'

Two weeks later, on 12 January 1836, a light air carried them towards the entrance of Port Jackson. They were astounded by the size of the town of Sydney, the large white stone houses, the windmills, the general air of prosperity. An acre of land in the centre of the town had just been sold for £12,000: 'an admirable country to grow rich in; turn shep-herd and I believe you must grow wealthy'. Following his usual custom, Darwin hired a man and two horses and set off inland. The roads were excellent, due largely to the iron gangs – parties of convicts working in chains under the guard of armed sentries – but there were few travellers except for the occasional bullock wagon piled up with bales of wool. He found the eucalyptus woods, with their pale foliage and shredding bark, desolate and untidy after his beloved tropical forests of South America; 'each side of the road is bordered by scrubby trees of the never-failing eucalyptus family', he says disparagingly. They gave no shade, a great disadvantage since he was riding in a temperature of 119°, in a wind which felt 'as though it had passed over a fire'. On his way back there was a pleasant interlude at a large country house outside Sydney, where he met a bevy of 'pretty, ladylike Australian girls – deliciously English-like'.

But Australia did not really interest him; he thought the scenery monotonous and disliked the state of society, supported by convict labour; how odious, he felt, to be waited on by a man who perhaps the day before had been flogged for some trifling misdemeanour and had no redress. He saw the convicts' lives being passed away with discontent and unhappiness, while the settlers were only bent on acquiring wealth.

228

An aborigine. FitzRoy was amazed at 'the lathy thinness of their persons, which seemed totally destitute of fat, and almost without flesh . . .' [N]

He reflected that nothing but 'rather sharp necessity' would compel him to emigrate.

No, the New World was not for Darwin. But the old world, the primaeval world of darkness of the aborigines and the prehistoric animals – that was a different matter. Far from being such utterly degraded beings as they had been represented, he found the aborigines to be good-humoured and pleasant, admirable in their own arts of tracking and throwing spears. He realised well enough that they had no future.

'Wherever the European has trod', he wrote, closely echoing Captain Cook, 'death seems to pursue the aboriginal'. Their numbers were already rapidly decreasing and they were becoming strangers and outcasts in their own country. 'It is very curious to see in the midst of a civilised people, a set of harmless savages wandering about without knowing where they shall sleep at night.' Even more disturbing was the fact that the aborigines seemed to accept this treatment without protest; they were all too grateful for the small help they got from the white man: the occasional use of his dogs for hunting, offal from his slaughterhouse, a little milk from his cows.

It was the same with the animals. He went kangaroo-hunting, riding for hours in the raging heat, but all the day long saw never a kangaroo nor even a wild dog. 'A few years since this country abounded with wild animals; but now the emu is banished to a long distance, and the kangaroo is become scarce; to both the English greyhound has been highly destructive. It may be long before these animals are altogether exterminated, but their doom is fixed.' He had one bit of luck; he saw several platypuses diving and playing in a river. 'Certainly it is a most extraordinary animal.'

But all in all Darwin was not sorry to leave Australia. By now homesickness had begun to overwhelm him; he only longed for England. He had been bitterly disappointed to find no letters awaiting him in Sydney; the last direct news he had had from his family was thirteen months old. He wrote to his sisters: 'I confess I never see a Merchant Vessel start for England, without a most dangerous inclination to bolt . . . I feel inclined to write about nothing else but to tell you, over and over again, how I long to be quietly seated among you . . . I am determined and feel sure that the scenery of England is ten times more beautiful than any we have seen . . . I have a constant longing, a feeling a prisoner would have . . . I feel inclined to keep up one steady deep growl from morning to night'. To Henslow: 'Oh the degree to which I long to be once again living quietly, with not one single novel object near me. No one can imagine it, till he has been whirled round the world, during 5 long years, in a ten Gun Brig'.

It was going to be nine long months before he reached home, but at least they were on their way. At the end of January the *Beagle* sailed for Hobart, in Tasmania, a six days' passage. From Hobart Darwin took the

ABOVE *Papeete harbour, Tahiti.* BELOW *Dawes Point, Sydney.* Watercolours by Conrad Martens.

ABOVE The Kangaroo dance. BELOW Another native dance, consisting 'in their running either sideways or in Indian file into an open space, and stamping the ground with great force as they marched together'. ¹

Head of an Australian aborigine.

opportunity to climb Mount Wellington, five and a half hours' hard climbing, a severe day's work, as he himself admitted. Again he was troubled by the treatment of the aborigines, who by then had all been chased out of their homes and removed to an island in Bass Straits, a 'most cruel step'. From Tasmania they went to King George's Sound, where they stayed for eight days: 'we did not during our voyage pass a more dull and uninteresting time', except for the lucky chance of witnessing a corroboree of the White Cockatoo tribe. 'It was a most rude, barbarous scene . . . but we observed that the black women and children watched it with the greatest pleasure . . . there was one [dance] called the Emu dance, in which each man extended his arm in a bent manner, like the neck of that bird. In another dance, one man imitated the movements of a kangaroo grazing in the woods, whilst a second crawled up, and pretended to spear him. When both tribes mingled in the dance, the ground trembled with the heaviness of their steps, and the air resounded with their wild cries . . . We have beheld many curious scenes in savage life, but never, I think, one where the natives were in such high spirits, and so perfectly at their ease.'

But this was the last of Australia. On 14 March the *Beagle* stood out of King George's Sound and for once Darwin permitted himself a piece of rhetoric: 'Farewell, Australia! you are a rising child . . . but you are too great and ambitious for affection, yet not great enough for respect. I leave your shores without sorrow or regret'.

The spring of 1836 found the *Beagle* pushing up through the Indian Ocean to the Cocos (or Keeling) Islands. If the Galapagos in appearance had been a kind of hell, then the Cocos were heaven; the dark ocean swell was breaking on the coral reef, boobies, frigate-birds and terns were wheeling over the coconut palms and the white sand beaches, and in the emerald-green water in the lagoons they could see gardens of brilliantly coloured coral. In bright moonlight the Malay women danced and sang for the sailors on the beach. By day the crew bathed and fished. They jumped on top of the turtles swimming in the lagoon and rode them to the shore, and they dragged up from the ocean floor great clams that were big enough to grasp a man's leg and hold him until he drowned. Darwin made several little excursions ashore with FitzRoy, and even the prosaic FitzRoy marvelled at the curiosities they saw: a coconut-eating crab, a coral-eating fish, dogs which caught fish, shells which became dangerous

Mount Wellington, Tasmania, which Darwin climbed, but which he found of little picturesque beauty. Altogether both he and FitzRoy were disappointed by the scenery of New Zealand and Australia.

man-traps; even rats making their nests at the top of high palm trees. Darwin observed the birds: boobies on their 'rude nests, stupid yet angry'; noddies, 'silly little creatures', and the small, snow-white terns, with large black eyes, which hovered a few feet above their heads: 'little imagination is required to fancy that so light and delicate a body must be tenanted by some wandering fairy spirit'.

There were huge crabs that fed on fallen coconuts. They were equipped with two strong pincers for tearing away the fibres of the bark covering the three eye-holes of the nut. This being done the crab would hammer open one of the holes and then turn round and with the aid of a secondary

235

pair of narrow pincers extract the meat: a marvellous example of a species adapting itself to its environment. 'As curious a case as ever I heard . . . of adaptation in structure between two objects so remote from each other in the scheme of nature as a crab and a coconut tree.' The islanders in their turn extracted the oil from the fat tail of the crab and would get as much as a pint and a half of oil from one crab.

It was in the Cocos islands that Darwin resolved another matter which had been on his mind for a long time. Back on the Chilean coast he had conceived the notion that if the crust of the earth could be elevated then it could also be depressed, that in fact while the Andes had been rising the floor of the Pacific Ocean had been gradually sinking. Already in October 1835, while they were on their way from the Galapagos to Tahiti, he had made a note on coral islands: ' . . . we saw several of those most curious rings of coral land, just rising above the water's edge, which have been called Lagoon Islands . . . These low hollow coral islands bear no proportion to the vast ocean out of which they abruptly rise; and it seems wonderful, that such weak invaders are not overwhelmed, by the all-powerful and never-tiring waves of that great sea, miscalled the Pacific'.

The three stages of coral development illustrated by section drawings of the same island. As the island subsides, the fringing reef builds up into a barrier reef and then becomes an atoll as the land itself sinks below sea-level.

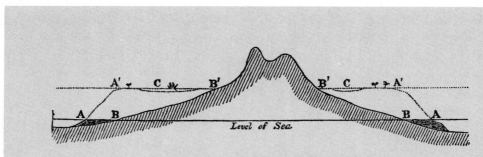

AA. Outer edges of the fringing-reef, at the level of the sea. BB. The shores of the fringed island.

A'A'. Outer edges of the reef, after its upward growth during a period of subsidence, now converted into a barrier, with islets on it. B'B'. The shores of the now encircled island. CC. Lagoon-channel.

N.B.—In this and the following woodcut, the subsidence of the land could be represented only by an apparent rise in the level of the sea.

Now was the time to test Lyell's theory that coral atolls represent coral-encrusted rims of submerged volcanic craters. Darwin believed that the coral polyp, the little animal that built up the reefs in tropical waters, would throw some light on the matter. The polyp could not live at a greater depth than 120 feet, and it had always been said that it had to perch itself close to a mainland shore or around volcanic islands. But suppose, he had asked himself, it was found that these reefs went down a very long way, and that all the coral below the 120-foot mark was dead – would not that be a proof that the floor of the ocean had been gradually sinking, and that the coral polyp had kept pace with this sinking by building the reefs up to the surface? This was a theory he could now put to the test.

He went out with FitzRoy in a small boat to the outer reef and carefully took numerous soundings on the steep outside of Keeling atoll. They found that up to the 120-foot mark the prepared tallow of the lead came up marked with the impression of living corals, but perfectly clean; as the depth increased the impressions became fewer, until at last it was evident that the bottom consisted of a smooth sandy layer. This suggested

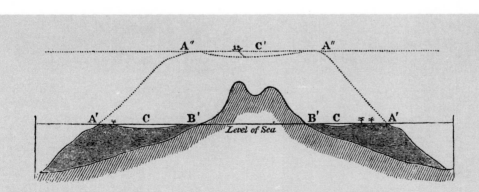

A′A′. Outer edges of the barrier-reef at the level of the sea, with islets on it. B′B′. The shores of the included island.   CC. The lagoon-channel.
A″A″. Outer edges of the reef, now converted into an atoll.   C′. The lagoon of the new atoll.
N.B.—According to the true scale, the depths of the lagoon-channel and lagoon are much exaggerated.

Port-Louis, capital of Mauritius. After his disappointment in the landscape of Australasia, Darwin found that 'the aspect of the island equalled the expectations raised by the many well-known descriptions of its beautiful scenery'. J

to Darwin that coral formations were the end products of aeons of slow reciprocal processes: the uplifting of an island by submarine volcanic action, the colonising of its slopes by myriad coral polyps, and finally the gradual subsiding of the island into the sea. He worked out that there were three different varieties of coral formations: atolls, barrier reefs and fringing reefs, all part of the same evolutionary process stretching over millions of years. The growth of the coral must keep pace with the

238

St Helena. 'It is a curious little world within itself; the habitable part is surrounded by a broad band of black desolate rocks, as if the wide barrier of the ocean was not sufficient to guard the precious spot.' [L]

subsidence beneath it, and so form first a barrier reef and then an atoll: 'Mountains of stone accumulated by the agency of various minute and tender animals'. He reckoned that the birth of an atoll required not less than a million years. As evidence of the subsidence of these reefs he noted the coconut trees falling in on all sides of the lagoon. 'In one place the foundation posts of a shed which the inhabitants asserted had stood 7 years just above high-water mark, was now daily washed by every tide.'

239

It was a dramatic and brilliant demonstration of his theory of the instability of the earth.

It was now late in the spring of 1836, and at last they could truly feel they were homeward bound. 'There never was a ship so full of homesick heroes as the *Beagle* . . . The Captain continues to push along with a slack rein and an armed heel.' When the weather was fine Darwin was busy getting his notes in order, and for the first time he was discovering the difficulties of expressing his ideas on paper. But he was in good spirits. FitzRoy too was busy all day writing, and the crew were well pleased with the good store of coconuts, poultry, pumpkins and turtles which the *Beagle* had taken on board at the Cocos Islands. On 29 April they reached Mauritius, an island 'adorned with an air of perfect elegance'. Darwin stayed for a couple of days with Captain Lloyd, the Surveyor General, who rather surprisingly sent him back to the ship on the back of his personal elephant, the only one on the island.

For the next two months they were rounding the Cape of Good Hope; they ran into rough weather and it became evident that their chances of reaching England before the end of the summer were receding; they put in only briefly at Cape Town but did not reach St Helena until 8 July. Darwin now had to face the fact that it would be October at the earliest before he got home. He found it hard to tolerate travelling any more; 'there is no country which has now any attractions for us, without it is seen right astern'. The five days they spent at St Helena were only made endurable for him by the walks which he took; he got lodgings within a stone's throw of Napoleon's tomb and wandered over the island from morning to night: 'I enjoyed these rambles more than I have done anything for a long time'. At Ascension Island, 'like a huge ship kept in first rate order', he got letters from home at last, and one of them told him that Professor Sedgwick had said that Charles Darwin 'should take a place among the leading scientific men'. This news, together with the sight of the volcanic rocks of Ascension, fired him again with all his old enthusiasm for geology. 'After reading this letter I clambered over the mountains with a bounding step, and made the volcanic rocks resound under my geological hammer.'

It was now nearly the end of July, and it was a bitter blow when FitzRoy decided that in order to complete his circle of chronological measurements of the world he must return home by way of South America.

ABOVE Entrance to Port-Jackson. BELOW Hobart Town, Tasmania.
OVERLEAF *A Bible-reading on board ship*, by Augustus Earle.

'This zig-zag manner of proceeding is very grievous; it has put the finishing touch to my feelings. I loathe, I abhor the sea, and all ships which sail on it. But yet I believe we shall reach England the latter half of October.' In point of fact things went better than this. They paused only a few days at Bahia and Pernambuco, and then on 19 August they left South America for the last time. The wind favoured them, and six weeks later the battered little *Beagle* sailed up the English Channel to her journey's end.

It was a Sunday, and in drenching rain FitzRoy held his last service on board to give thanks to God for their safe return. In this at least Darwin could fervently join him; he was frantic to get home to his family and his cousins in Maer Hall. 'On the 2nd of October we made the shores of England; and at Falmouth I left the *Beagle*, having lived on board the good little vessel nearly five years.'

Heads of natives of New Zealand and King George's Sound, drawn by FitzRoy.

ABOVE The platypus (*Ornithorhynchus anatinus*). BELOW The King Island emu, now extinct (*Dromiceius diemenianus*).

Darwin in 1853. Chalk drawing by Samuel Lawrence.

CHAPTER XII

THE OXFORD MEETING

Darwin did not lose any time in making for home. As soon as the *Beagle* was tied up in the harbour at Falmouth he hurried ashore and took the first coach for Shrewsbury, where he arrived two days later, on 4 October. But it was quite late in the evening when the coach got into the town, and with all his eagerness to be home and to see his family again he was too kind-hearted, too disciplined perhaps, to think of disturbing them at such an hour. He slept the night at an inn, and the next morning walked into The Mount, unannounced, just as his father and sisters were sitting down to breakfast. Amid all the cries of welcome Dr Darwin turned to his daughters and said: 'Why, the shape of his head is quite altered'.

One incident pleased Charles immensely. He went into the yard and called for his dog, as he had been accustomed to do every morning in the past. The dog came out and set off ahead on their usual walk, showing no more emotion or excitement than if it had been yesterday, instead of five years ago, that they had last walked together.

Almost immediately Darwin wrote off to his uncle Josiah Wedgwood: 'My head is quite confused with so much delight', and his cousin Emma wrote, 'We are getting impatient for Charles's arrival'.

Darwin saw the ship once more; in May 1837 he wrote, 'I have been paying the *Beagle* a visit today. She sails in a week for Australia. It appeared marvellously odd to see the little vessel and to think that I should not be one of the party. If it was not for the seasickness, I should have no objection to start again'.

He never did start again, however; it seems almost impossible to believe, but Darwin, though he lived till the age of seventy-three, never again left the shores of England. This was largely due to the fact that from 1838 onwards the life of this adventurous and seemingly robust young man, still only twenty-nine years old, was dominated by ill-health. In 1842 he made a trip to Wales: 'This excursion . . . was the last time I was ever strong enough to climb mountains or to take long walks'. His son Francis in his reminiscences of his father wrote: 'For nearly forty years he never knew one day of the health of ordinary men, and thus his life was one long struggle against the weariness and strain of sickness'. The nature of his illness has never been clearly established; the terrible bouts of seasickness he suffered on the voyage may have played a part. Some doctors, leaning on the rather critical and authoritarian character of Darwin's father, have suggested that the illness was psycho-somatic; others thought he must indeed have caught Chagas's disease from that Benchuga bug with which he experimented in South America. Probably Julian Huxley's answer is the reasonable one: that he suffered from a combination of psycho-neurotic ill-health and some infection (again possibly Chagas's disease) contracted while on the voyage. Whatever it was, we cannot doubt Darwin's words when he said in 1871, 'I never pass 24 hours without many hours of discomfort'.

But in 1836, freshly released from the confined spaces of the *Beagle*, he threw himself into such a passion of activity that he had no time to think of his health. These were the two most active years of his life. He set to work to classify his enormous collection of specimens, hurrying between Cambridge and London and Shrewsbury. At first it was not easy to get the experts to help him; 'I have not made much progress with the great men; I find, as you told me, that they are all overwhelmed with their own business', he wrote to Henslow a month after he got back. But Henslow himself, and Lyell, were endlessly encouraging, and through their influence he got a grant of £1000 towards a five-volume work on the zoology of the *Beagle,* which he edited, and he was made Secretary of the Geological Society of London. He was also busy writing his *Journal of the Voyage of the Beagle,* which was first published in 1839 as Volume III of the three-volume narrative of the surveying voyages of HMS *Adventure* and HMS *Beagle.*

In 1837 Darwin took rooms in London near his brother Erasmus, and at the end of January 1839 he married his cousin Emma, youngest daughter of Josiah Wedgwood, his favourite Uncle Jos. Emma was a charming woman, a year older than Darwin, intelligent and gay and very musical; she had had piano lessons from Chopin. Her aunt, Madame Sismondi, said of her that she would 'lark it through life', and although this does not seem to have been very likely, seeing that she had ten children and a husband who was a constant invalid, nonetheless she was clearly an excellent wife. Few husbands would write as Darwin did, thirty years later: 'I can declare that in my whole life I have not heard her utter one word which I had rather had been unsaid'. She on her side described him as 'the most open, transparent man I ever saw, and every word expresses his real thoughts. He is particularly affectionate and very nice to his father and sisters, and perfectly sweet-tempered, and possesses some minor qualities that add particularly to one's happiness – such as being humane to animals'. She found it impossible to enter into his work, and did not even find it interesting to watch his experiments, but she never made any pretence about it. Once when they attended a scientific lecture together he said to her, 'I am afraid this is very wearisome to you'. 'Not more than all the rest', she said. He used to quote this with pleasure; they evidently understood one another perfectly.

When they were first married the Darwins lived in Gower Street, in London, but by 1842 Charles could not take the strain of a city life, and they moved to Down House in Kent, sixteen miles outside London.

LEFT Erasmus Alvey Darwin. Sketch by George Richmond. 'He was extremely agreeable and his wit often reminded me of that in the letters and works of Charles Lamb.' [A] RIGHT Emma Darwin. After a portrait by George Richmond. When Darwin was making up his mind whether to marry or not, he wrote to himself on a scrap of paper: 'Only picture to yourself a nice, soft wife on a sofa with good fire, and books and music perhaps – compare this with the dingy reality of Gt Malboro' St. [where he had lodgings] Marry – Marry – Marry'

Down House from the back. 'It is not . . . quite so retired a place as a writer in a German periodical makes it, who says that my house can be approached only by a mule-track!' [A]

At first he visited London every two or three weeks, hoping 'not to turn into a Kentish hog', but soon he found even this too much for him, and gradually he settled down into a routine which was not to alter for the rest of his life. His hours of scientific work were invariable: 8 to 9.30 a.m., and 10.30 to midday; by then he considered his 'work' for the day done. The writing up of his material was for him the worst part; he found it an exacting and painful labour. The rest of his time was spent in walking, riding, resting, thinking, answering letters, and long hours of reading. 'When I see the list of books of all kinds which I read and abstracted', he wrote later, 'I am surprised at my industry'. His library became large, but above all it was a working library; for books in themselves he had no feeling, and when studying a heavy book would sometimes tear it in half to make it easier to handle. Weekdays and Sundays passed by alike, each with their stated intervals of work and rest.

This period of his life was occupied with immediate matters: editing the five volumes of the *Zoology of the Beagle,* working on a paper on coral reefs, which took him twenty hard months, and endlessly revising and correcting his material from the voyage of the *Beagle.* John Murray, the publisher, read the *Journal* when it came out in 1839, and realised at once that, apart from its scientific value, it was one of the best books of travel and adventure ever written. He bought up the unsold stock, bound up a few copies and sent them round to some influential friends. When he found that they were as enthusiastic about the book as he was he bought the copyright for £150 and put it out again in 1845. From then on it had a steadily increasing sale, and was finally translated and published all over the world. Darwin was delighted: 'the success of this my first literary child always tickles my vanity more than that of my other books'.

By 1846 he thought he was finished with the *Beagle.* In October he wrote to Henslow: 'You cannot think how delighted I am at having finished all my *Beagle* materials . . . it is now 10 years since my return, and your words, which I thought preposterous, are come true, that it would take twice the number of years to describe, that it took to collect and observe'. In fact there was one item left over from the voyage, a tiny cirripede or barnacle, not much bigger than the head of a pin, and the study and classification of this species took up the next eight years of Darwin's life.

ABOVE Sea perches (*Plectropomidae*) from King George's Sound. BELOW Baby Australian sea-lion (*Neophoca cinerea*).

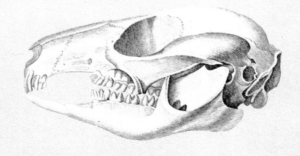

Now his work stretched before him with ever wider horizons. He had so many ideas; he was interested in everything. He studied sheep, cattle, pigs, dogs, cats, poultry, peacocks, canaries, goldfish, earthworms, bees and silk moths, as well as flowers and vegetables. He particularly experimented with pigeons and joined two pigeon fanciers' clubs; the men called him 'Squire' and he sat at their meetings in a cloud of tobacco smoke. One of his fellow members wrote about a certain pigeon: 'If it was possible for noblemen and gentlemen to know the amazing amount of solace and pleasure derived from the Almond Tumbler . . . scarce any nobleman or gentleman would be without their aviaries.' Darwin completely agreed with him: 'Pigeon raising is a majestic and noble pursuit and beats moths and butterflies, whatever you say to the contrary'.

He had a great love for experiment – 'I shan't be easy till I've tried it' – and much enjoyed what he called fool's experiments; once, for instance, he asked his son Francis to play his bassoon close to the leaves of a sensitive plant; he fancied it might vibrate to the chords.

One does not readily believe that the pleasures of Victorian family life were as idyllic as biographers make out. But in the Darwins' case there is no doubt whatever; parents, children, relations, friends, acquaintances – all have left undisputed evidence of a genuine happy family. Maria Edgeworth described Charles's 'radiantly cheerful countenance'. Another visitor wrote that 'when Charles is most unwell he continues sociable and affectionate'. 'More than any woman I ever knew, she *comforted*', said Mrs Huxley about Emma. Darwin had an altogether exceptional devotion to his children, treating them with an affection and kindness which they never forgot. Perhaps this was in some part a reaction against the rather authoritative treatment he had received from his own father; in any case, he treated them from the first as independent human beings, a rare approach to children in those days. The Darwins had ten children, seven of whom survived childhood, and they never had the least fear of their father. One of them at four years old tried to bribe him with sixpence to play with them during his working hours. If a child was ill it might easily be found tucked up on the sofa in his study 'for comfort and company'.

He wrote the most charming, warm-hearted letters; when his eldest son Willy got a good place at Rugby: 'My dear old Willy, I have not for a very long time been more pleased than I was this morning at receiving

The wallaby, or short-tailed kangaroo (*Setonix brachyurus*).

The New study at Down House.

your letter with the *excellent* news . . . We are so very glad to hear that
you are happy and comfortable . . . I go my morning walk and often think
of you'. To his son George when he was appointed second Wrangler at
Cambridge: 'My dear old fellow . . . Again and again I congratulate
you . . . You have made my hand tremble so I can scarcely write'. He was
present at the death of his second daughter Annie when she died in
Malvern at the age of ten (Emma could not be there because she was
about to have her ninth child), and still twenty-five years afterwards
tears would come into his eyes when he thought about her.

The Darwins were a comparatively wealthy family; when his father died Charles inherited £5000 a year. He was most liberal with money to all his children; he balanced his accounts at the end of each year and divided the surplus among them.

Except for family visits, Darwin took few holidays; the only breaks were made when he had to go off for several weeks at a time to take the 'water-cure', the one thing that seemed to improve his health. As his work took a deeper and deeper hold on him other interests faded, and became even actively irritating. Writing in 1876 he said that he 'could not endure to read a line of poetry . . . found Shakespeare intolerably dull, and music merely drove his thoughts to worry about his work'. The one thing that really entertained him was listening to a book being read aloud, preferably a novel with a happy ending. This was the man who at Cambridge had organised Shakespeare readings in his room, had taken the greatest pleasure in listening to Mozart and Beethoven and had invariably carried a volume of Milton's poems in his pocket on his inland expeditions in South America. He himself found this 'curious and lamentable loss of the higher aesthetic tastes' very odd. But there it was; 'My chief enjoyment and sole employment throughout life has been scientific work'.

This way of life naturally did not bring him into much contact with

Bald head (LEFT) and pouter pigeons. Drawings at Down House.

FitzRoy, and in fact the two men did not meet again often once the voyage was over. In 1843 FitzRoy was appointed Governor and Commander-in-Chief of New Zealand, but his obvious partiality for the aborigines – no doubt his missionary instincts at work – made him unpopular with the settlers and the Admiralty soon recalled him. It was not long before he retired from the Navy, though he was moved up to Vice-Admiral on their books. But while the course of Darwin's life – always with the exception of his health – was a steady upward progression, poor FitzRoy's circumstances and character combined to frustrate and depress him. His first wife died in 1852, and four years later his eldest daughter also, a beautiful girl of sixteen. In 1857 he applied for the post of Chief Naval Officer in the Board of Trade's maritime department, but it was given instead to Sulivan – the man who twenty-five years before had been his second lieutenant in the *Beagle*. For a man of FitzRoy's pride this must have been hard to accept. He became a great expert on weather prediction; in fact he was the originator of all the weather forecasting on which shipping now depends. But here again he came in for criticism, *The Times* going so far as to refer to 'the singularly uncouth and obscure dialect employed by the Admiral in his explanations'. This time he had not got the support and loyalty of his comrades on the *Beagle* which had brought him out of the same sort of lowness of spirit so many years before.

Gradually as their views diverged – Darwin becoming more and more engrossed in his scientific theories, FitzRoy more and more convinced of the literal truth of every word in the Bible – they became less than friends, and their last meeting in 1857, when FitzRoy went to stay at Down House for two nights, was not a success; FitzRoy was a man, Darwin wrote to his sister, 'who has the most consummate skill in looking at everything and everybody in a perverted manner'.

But now the great crisis – and glory – of Darwin's life was coming upon him. All these years, ever since he had seen the Galapagos Islands and had started classifying and correlating his materials from the voyage of the *Beagle*, he had been 'haunted' – his own word – by the conviction that the various species of life on earth had diverged from ancestral lines; they had not been created complete and unchanging, heredity and environment had produced new forms. Far back in 1837 he had started his first notebook – later to become a series of notebooks – on the mutation of species, and when a year later he read Malthus's book *An Essay on the Principle of Population* (which had been first published in 1798) he felt certain that he was on the track of an idea of great importance; so much so that a few years later he made a rough outline of his theory and left it with a letter to his wife asking her to publish it in the event of his sudden death.

He took no steps towards publishing it himself, however; he must have realised what a storm these heretical ideas would arouse. He tells us in his autobiography that as a young man, before going to Cambridge, he did not 'in the least doubt the strict and literal truth of the Bible', and he recalled that even later, while on board the *Beagle*, he had been heartily laughed at by several of the officers for 'quoting the Bible as an unanswerable authority on some points of morality'. It cannot have been easy for him to accept his own discoveries; his religious upbringing must have put up a great fight against the conclusions he was forced to draw. But he knew he was right. 'Disbelief crept over me at a very slow rate but was at last complete. The rate was so slow that I felt no distress, and have never since doubted even for a single second that my conclusion was correct.'

His conclusion, as he expanded it later, was briefly this: 'As many more individuals of each species are born than can possibly survive, and as consequently there is a frequently recurring struggle for existence, it follows that any being, if it vary however slightly in any manner profitable to itself . . . will have a better chance of surviving, and thus be naturally selected . . . This preservation of favourable individual differences and variations, and the destruction of those which are injurious, I have called Natural Selection, or the Survival of the Fittest'.

His description of the army ants which he had watched twenty years before in the rain forest in Brazil, and his deductions from their behaviour, made a basis for all future scientific research on the subject. 'In this case,' he wrote, 'selection has been applied to the family and not to the individual, for the sake of gaining a serviceable end'. This end was the good of the colony, within which there are really no individuals; each ant, deaf and almost sightless, functioned as one cell in a giant organism, powered by blind instinct. He remembered also the insects he had observed in the same forest, and the way they had used camouflage as a means of protection. 'Assuming that an insect originally happened to resemble in some degree a dead twig or a decayed leaf, and that it varied slightly in many ways, then all the variations which rendered the insects more like any such object would be preserved, whilst other variations would be ultimately lost; or if they rendered the insect less like the imitated object, they would be eliminated.'

There was also the factor of sexual selection, selection operating through advantages in the struggle for reproduction; 'beauty', he wrote later, 'is sometimes better than success in battle'. The accumulation of favourable variations over long periods of time must result in the emergence of new species and the extinction of older ones.

Here was heresy. To the average Christian every word in the Bible was still literally true. In Britain Archbishop Ussher and Dr John Lightfoot of Cambridge University by a series of mystical calculations had fixed the actual date of the creation of the world – it was at 9 a.m. on Sunday 23 October in 4004 B.C. – and this extraordinary pronouncement was printed with all the authority of the Gospel itself in many copies of the Bible that were in circulation at the time. There was much theological argument about the exact interpretation of the Bible, but the facts of the Book of Genesis were sacrosanct: the world had been created by God in six days, man had been made in His image, all the creatures of the earth had sprung into existence at the same instant, and had survived the Flood only because Noah had taken two of each species, a male and a female, aboard the Ark.

It might be argued, of course, that many people still believe these things today, but in Victorian England they were at the very heart of nearly everyone's consciousness, they were as definite and unchallengeable as night and day; if you took these foundations away you destroyed society, you mocked God Himself. No wonder Darwin had delayed for more than twenty years before publishing his heretical theories on the origin of the teeming species on earth; in England he faced social ostracism, on the Continent he might easily have been arrested, a little earlier the Inquisition would certainly have had him.

He would have waited even longer had he not been in danger of being forestalled by another naturalist, Alfred Russel Wallace, who was thinking upon the same lines as himself. In June 1858 there had arrived out of the blue a letter to Darwin from Wallace, enclosing an essay and asking Darwin, if he thought it good enough, to send it on to Lyell. The essay was entitled *On the Tendencies of Varieties to Depart Indefinitely from the Original Type*.

Darwin, as usual, behaved admirably. Faced with the prospect of his years of work being rendered worthless, his brilliant new theory anticipated, he did not hesitate for a moment. He sent the essay on to Lyell with a warm recommendation. 'So all my originality', he could not help adding, 'will be smashed'.

Fortunately both Lyell and Joseph Hooker knew of all the work he had already done on the subject, and had read his outline of his theories, and they persuaded him that he must not step aside; he and Wallace must act together. It was arranged that a joint paper should be presented to the Linnean Society the following month.

A year later Darwin published his book, *On the Origin of Species by means of Natural Selection, or the preservation of favoured races in the struggle for life*. It was put out by John Murray, and the first edition of 1250 copies sold out on the day of publication. Surprisingly there was not a great deal of fuss at first. Most scientists sniffed at the theory cautiously, and except for a few who took sides, preferred to reserve their judgement; as Hooker said later, 'the interest aroused was intense, but the subject was too novel and too ominous for the old school to enter the lists unarmed'.

But it was too revolutionary an issue to lie dormant, it pushed at men's minds everywhere. What Darwin was saying, or at any rate suggesting, was that the world had not been created in a week, and certainly not in the year 4004 B.C. It was inconceivably older than this, it had changed out of recognition and was still changing, all living creatures had changed as well, and man, far from being made in God's image, may have begun as something much more primitive. The story of Adam and Eve, in brief, was a myth.

This was intolerable. People were furious at the idea that they might share a common lineage with animals. They thought, wrongly, that he was saying that man had descended from an ape; in fact, what he did believe was that modern man and modern apes had diverged in prehistory from a common line of ancestors.

As long ago as 1844 Darwin had written to Hooker: 'At last gleams of light have come, and I am almost convinced (quite contrary to the opinion I started with) that species are not (it is like confessing a murder) immutable'. Now the murder was out. It was not possible any longer for the Church to stand aside. By 1860, when Darwin's book had run through three editions, the clergy were thoroughly aroused, and they chose to come out and do battle at that famous meeting of the British Association which was held at Oxford in June that year, the meeting which was to bring together the great exponents of science and religion to debate the theory of the origin of the species.

There is something anachronistic, even absurd, about the whole controversy; it seems to belong, not to the last century, but to the Middle Ages, and one has to make a conscious effort of the mind to believe that it really happened. There were of course many scientists, especially geologists, who had moved a long way towards the theory of evolution themselves: Darwin's grandfather, Erasmus Darwin, Buffon and Lamarck, and others such as Henry Adams who felt 'an instinctive belief in evolution'. But nonetheless most of Darwin's contemporaries were content to accept Paley's theory that the form of every existing species of plant and animal bore unmistakable witness to the divine hand.

The clergy arrived at the meeting in strength; they were led by the formidable figure of Samuel Wilberforce, the Bishop of Oxford, a man whose impassioned eloquence was a little too glib for some people (he was known as 'Soapy Sam'), but whose influence was very great indeed. Wilberforce announced beforehand that he was out to 'smash Darwin'. He was supported by the anatomist Richard Owen, who was a rabid anti-Darwinist, and who probably supplied the Bishop with scientific ammunition for his speech. Darwin was ill and could not come, but his old teacher, Professor Henslow, was in the chair, and he had two ardent champions in T. H. Huxley and the botanist Hooker.

Things got off to a slow start. Through Thursday, 28 June, and Friday, the discussion droned on among minor scientists in a desultory way. By a coincidence FitzRoy had come to the meeting to read a paper on *British Storms,* and this he did on the Friday. But by the Saturday it was known that Soapy Sam was ready, and so many people crowded into the meeting – undergraduates as well as the clergy and the scientists and their wives – that it had to be moved from the usual Lecture Room in the Library to the New University Museum.

The proceedings opened quietly, not to say dully. For an hour or more Professor Draper from America rambled on about the 'intellectual development of Europe considered with reference to the views of Mr Darwin and others', and he was followed by three other speakers who were hardly more inspired. The last of them, a man with an odd accent, began making diagrams on the blackboard. 'Let this point A be the man', he declared, and 'let that point B be the mawnkey'. This was too much for the bored undergraduates. They had come to be entertained and entertainment they were going to have, even if they had to generate it themselves. 'Mawnkey, Mawnkey', they roared, and refused to allow the unfortunate speaker to continue.

By now Wilberforce had entered the hall with his attendant clergy about him, and he created something of a stir with his priestly clothes and his air of confident episcopal authority. Henslow called on him to speak, and he plunged at once with a fine flow of words into ridicule of Darwin's 'Casual theory'. Where were the proofs? Darwin was merely expressing sensational opinions, and they went flatly against the divine revelation of the Bible. This was no more than had been expected, but the Bishop on rising to the height of his peroration went too far. He turned to Huxley, who was sitting on the platform – an arresting figure in his top-coat, his high wing collar and his leonine black hair – and demanded to know if it was through his grandmother or his grandfather that he claimed to be descended from the apes.

It was not really the moment for heavy sarcasm, and Huxley was not a man to provoke lightly.* It was by chance that he was at the meeting at all; he had met a friend in the street that morning who had persuaded him to go. Now when he heard how ignorantly the Bishop presented his case, ending with his 'insolent question', he said in an undertone, 'The Lord hath delivered him into my hands'. He got up and announced that he would certainly prefer to be descended from an ape rather than from a cultivated man who prostituted the gifts of culture and eloquence to the service of prejudice and falsehood. The Bishop in short did not know what he was talking about.

One did not lightly insult the clergy in the 1860s. Uproar ensued. The undergraduates clapped and shouted, the clergy angrily demanded an apology, and the ladies from their seats under the windows fluttered their handkerchiefs in consternation. One of them, a Lady Brewster, collapsed from shock and had to be carried out.

---

*Years later, when Samuel Butler attacked Darwin in a series of letters, Huxley quoted Goethe's lapidary phrase: 'Every whale has its louse'.

LEFT Samuel Wilberforce, Bishop of Oxford. RIGHT T. H. Huxley. Caricatures by 'Ape' in *Vanity Fair*, at the time of the Oxford meeting.

LEFT Charles Darwin. RIGHT Richard Owen. Caricatures from *Vanity Fair*.

And now something intensely interesting intervened. Amid the hubbub a slight grey-haired man got to his feet. His thin aristocratic face was clouded with rage, and he waved a Bible aloft like an avenging prophet. Here was the truth, he cried, here and nowhere else. Long ago he had warned Darwin about his dangerous thoughts. Had he but known then that he was carrying in his ship such a . . . He was shouted down and the rest of his words were lost.

There were those in the audience who recognised Vice-Admiral Robert FitzRoy, and it must have been a disturbing thing to hear him so passionately denouncing his old shipmate. Indeed, it was both disturbing and a little shocking, for it carried the memory back to the beginning of this whole affair, to the days when FitzRoy and Darwin were eager young men in their twenties, both delighting in one another's company, both utterly engrossed in their great adventure – the five years' voyage of the *Beagle*.

It was on that voyage that Darwin had first begun to explore his ideas about evolution, and FitzRoy, unconsciously, had helped him by arguing with him. Stage by stage as they had travelled round the world young Darwin had pitted his notions against the blank wall of FitzRoy's uncompromising faith – it had been like battering down the Church itself – and by that very opposition had been encouraged to persist in his enquiries, to embark on that other long, hard, speculative journey of the mind.

Now, thirty years later, it must have been a bitter experience for FitzRoy to stand up in this noisy crowded room and hear Darwin's name acclaimed. It was turning white into black. How had it happened? How had these satanic thoughts prevailed? Hurt, bewildered and furious, he went out, and it was less than five years later that in a spasm of annihilating and righteous despair he committed suicide.

'I often doubt what will be his [FitzRoy's] end', Darwin had written to his sister Susan as long ago as 1836; 'under many circumstances I am sure it would be a brilliant one, under others I fear a very unhappy one'. FitzRoy cut his throat on a Sunday morning, 30 April 1865; he was fifty-nine years old.

Darwin lived on for another twenty-two years after the Oxford meeting, and his health somewhat improved. The *Origin of Species* was published in many editions all over the world, and he wrote eight more major works,

MONKEYANA.

Am I satyr or man?
Pray tell me who can,
And settle my place in the scale.
A man in ape's shape,
An anthropoid ape,
Or monkey deprived of his tail?

The *Vestiges* taught,
That all came from naught
By "development," so called, "progressive;"
That insects and worms
Assume higher forms
By modification excessive.

Then DARWIN set forth,
In a book of much worth,
The importance of "Nature's selection;"
How the struggle for life
Is a laudable strife,
And results in "specific distinction."

Let pigeons and doves
Select their own loves,
And grant them a million of ages,
Then doubtless you'll find
They've altered their kind,
And changed into prophets and sages.

LEONARD HORNER relates,
That Biblical dates
The age of the world cannot trace;
That Bible tradition,
By Nile's deposition,
Is put to the right about face.

Then there's PENGELLY
Who next will tell ye
That he and his colleagues of late
Find celts and shaped stones
Mixed up with cave bones
Of contemporaneous date.

Then PRESTWICH, he pelts
With hammers and celts
All who do not believe his relation,
That the tools he exhumes
From gravelly tombs
Date before the Mosaic creation.

Then HUXLEY and OWEN,
With rivalry glowing,
With pen and ink rush to the scratch;
'Tis Brain *versus* Brain,
Till one of them 's siain;
By Jove! it will be a good match!

Says OWEN, you can see
The brain of Chimpanzee
Is always exceedingly small,
With the hindermost "horn"
Of extremity shorn,
And no "Hippocampus" at all.

The Professor then tells 'em,
That man's "cerebellum,"
From a vertical point you can't see;
That each "convolution"
Contains a solution,
Of "Archencephalic" degree

Then apes have no nose,
And thumbs for great toes,
And a pelvis both narrow and slight;
They can't stand upright,
Unless to show fight,
With "DU CHAILLU," that chivalrous knight!

Next HUXLEY replies,
That OWEN he lies,
And garbles his Latin quotation;
That his facts are not new,
His mistakes not a few,
Detrimental to his reputation.

"To twice slay the slain,"
By dint of the Brain,
(Thus HUXLEY concludes his review)
Is but labour in vain,
Unproductive of gain,
And so I shall bid you "Adieu!"

Zoological Gardens, May, 1861.   GORILLA.

PUNCH'S ESSENCE OF PARLIAMENT.

MONDAY, *May* 6. The Lords had a discussion about the Canal of the Future, that is to say, the impossible trench which M. LESSEPS pretends to think he can cut through the Isthmus of Suez. The Government opinion upon the subject is, that if the Canal could be made, we ought not, for political reasons, to allow it, but that inasmuch as the Canal cannot be cut, the subject may, and the wise course is to let the speculators ruin themselves and diddle the Pacha. This seems straightforward and benevolent enough.

MR. SPEAKER DENISON, who had had a relapse into indisposition, re-appeared, and made his apologies for having been ill. The House cheered him so loudly that he began to think he had done a clever thing, rather than not, in catching the rheumatism. *Mr. Punch* hopes to behold the brave Speaker "astir in his saddle" (as MR. DISRAELI's song goes) in due season, and to see him, like a true Whig, following Fox and avoiding pit.

LORD JOHN RUSSELL made an important reply to an important question from MR. GREGORY. The American Difficulty is beginning to create English difficulties. The North is calling on PRESIDENT LINCOLN to blockade the ports of the South, and the South is sending out Privateers to intercept the commerce of the North. LORD JOHN announced that England can recognise no blockade except a real one, and that she is prepared to regard the South as sufficiently consolidated to entitle her to be treated as a Belligerent, not as a mere rebel, and therefore her right to issue letters of marque must be acknowledged. This is a very prosaic paragraph, but *Mr. Punch* "reserves to himself" the right to be grave, gay, lively, and severe exactly when it pleases him.

Our Daughter ALICE is to have £30,000 down, and £6,000 a year, LORD PALMERSTON remarking, very properly, that she is not our Eldest Daughter, and may not require the same allowance as the future QUEEN OF PRUSSIA, but that it is not for the honour of England that her Princesses should go out as paupers. Quite the reverse, and what is more, *Mr. Punch* insists that all the money be settled on his amiable young friend ALICE, so that she may draw her own cheques, and not have to ask her husband for money every time she wants to buy pins or postage stamps, or a little present to send over to her dear *Mr. Punch.*

Then was the Paper Resolution moved by MR. GLADSTONE. LORD ROBERT CECIL opposed it, and hoped the Lords would reject the Bill to be based on it: MR. LEVESON GOWER approved it, and paraded the

Parody in *Punch* of the Wedgwood anti-slavery cameo.

Charles Darwin

Henrietta (Mrs Lichfield) and William Darwin

Emma Darwin

Sir Francis Darwin

Major Leonard Darwin

Elizabeth Darwin

Sir George Darwin

Sir Horace Darwin

Darwin, his wife and members of their family.

Darwin as an old man. In the winter of 1882, at the age of 73, he wrote to a friend, 'my course is nearly run'.

including the pre-eminently important *The Descent of Man*. His reputation grew steadily; he was given an honorary doctor's degree at Cambridge, and when he attended a lecture at the Royal Institution the whole assembly rose to their feet and applauded him. Down House is now a museum, and there are Darwin museums and libraries all over the world, including Moscow; a mountain range in the Cordilleras, has taken his name. On the Galapagos Islands there is a biological research station maintained by the Charles Darwin Foundation.

Charles Darwin is now recognised as the man who, as Julian Huxley says, 'provided a foundation for the entire structure of modern biology', but during his lifetime he received no official honour from the State (though three of his sons were later knighted). The Church was strong enough to see to that. He never stopped working. 'When I am obliged to give up observation and experiment', he said, 'I shall die'. He was working on 17 April 1882; he died two days later. He was buried at Westminster Abbey, with Huxley, Hooker and Wallace among the pall-bearers.

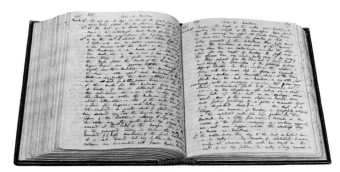

Manuscript of Darwin's journal of the voyage of the *Beagle*.

Australian and Mauritian squids (*Sepiadariidae*).

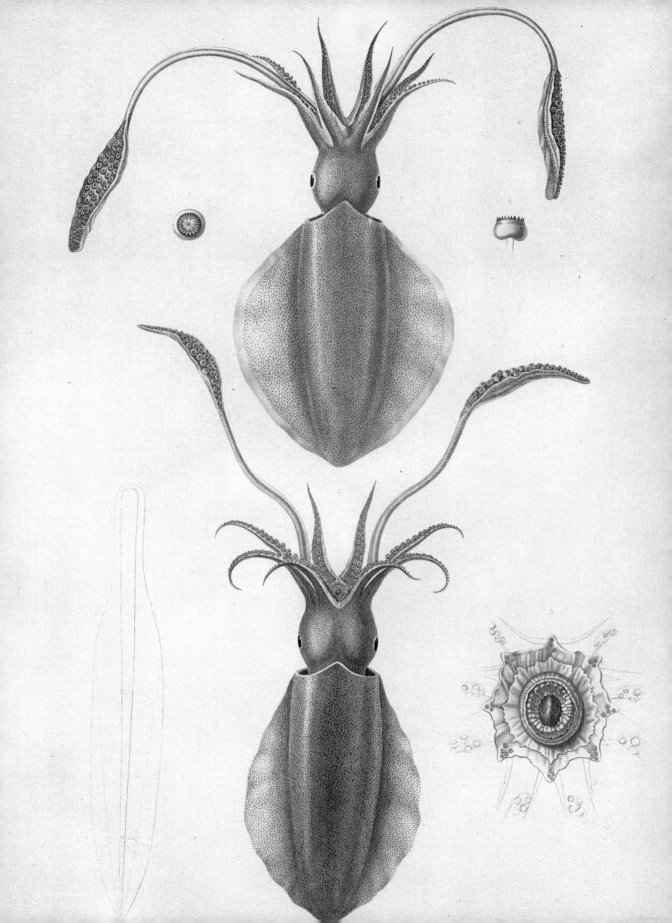

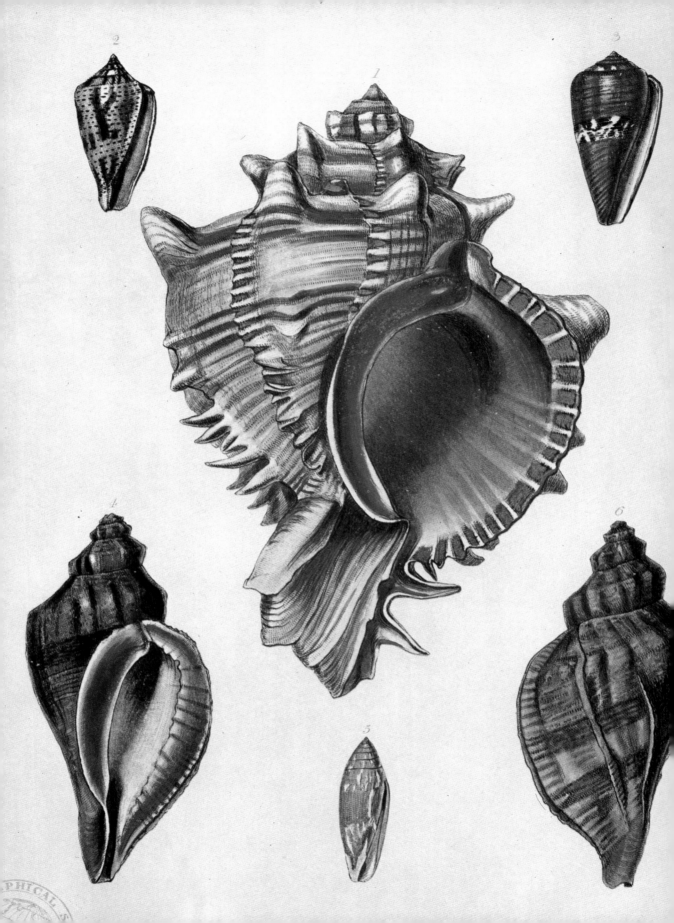

CHRONOLOGY OF THE VOYAGE

The matter in roman type refers to the major ports of call of the *Beagle*; the matter in *italic type* refers to some of Darwin's most important inland excursions.

1831—**27 December** Departure from Devonport.

1832
- **18 January to 8 February** Cape Verde Islands.
- **28 February to 18 March** Bahia.
- **4 April to 5 July** Rio de Janeiro.
- **8 to 23 April** *Excursions to various estates inland.*
- **26 July to 19 August** Montevideo.
- **6 September to 17 October** Bahia Blanca.
- **2 to 26 November** Montevideo.
- **16 December to 26 February 1833** Tierra del Fuego.

1833
- **1 March to 6 April** Falkland Islands.
- **28 April to 23 July** Maldonado.
- **3 to 24 August** Mouth of the Rio Negro.
- **11 to 17 August** *Excursion from El Carmen to Bahia Blanca.*
- **24 August to 6 October** surveying the Argentinian coast.
- **8 to 20 September** *Excursion from Bahia Blanca to Buenos Aires.*
- **6 to 19 October** Maldonado.
- **27 September to 20 October** *Excursion to Santa Fé and along the Parana.*
- **21 October to 6 December** Montevideo.
- **14 to 28 November** *Excursion to Mercedes.*

1834
- **23 December to 4 January 1834** Port Desire.
- **9 to 19 January** Port Saint Julian.
- **29 January to 7 March** Tierra del Fuego.
- **10 March to 7 April** Falkland Islands.
- **13 April to 12 May** Santa Cruz river.
- **18 April to 8 May** *Excursion up the Santa Cruz river.*
- **28 June to 13 July** Chiloe.

1834
- **31 July to 10 November** Valparaiso.
- **14 August to 27 September** *Excursion into the Andes.*

1835
- **21 November to 4 February 1835** Chiloe and Chonos archipelago.
- **8 to 22 February** Valdivia.
- **4 to 7 March** Concepcion.
- **11 to 17 March** Valparaiso.
- **13 March to 10 April** *Excursion from Santiago, across the Andes to Mendoza.*
- **27 March to 17 April** neighbourhood of Concepcion.
- **17 April to 27 June** Chilean coast.
- **27 April to 4 July** *Excursion to Coquimbo and Copiapo.*
- **12 to 15 July** Iquiqui (Peru).
- **19 July to 7 September** Callao.
- **16 September to 20 October** Galapagos Islands.
- **15 to 26 November** Tahiti.
- **21 to 30 December** New Zealand.

1836
- **12 to 30 January** Sydney.
- **2 to 17 February** Hobart, Tasmania.
- **3 to 14 March** King George's Sound.
- **2 to 12 April** Cocos (Keeling) Islands.
- **29 April to 9 May** Mauritius.
- **31 May to 18 June** Cape of Good Hope.
- **7 to 14 July** St Helena.
- **19 to 23 July** Ascencion Island.
- **1 to 6 August** Bahia.
- **12 to 17 August** Pernambuco.
- **2 October** Arrival at Falmouth.

Murex shells and cones.

BIBLIOGRAPHY

Barlow, Nora (Ed.) *Charles Darwin and the Voyage of the 'Beagle'*, New York, 1945. *Darwin and Henslow : the growth of an idea. Letters 1831–1860*, London, 1967.

Darwin, Charles *Narrative of the Surveying Voyages of HMS 'Adventure' and 'Beagle' between 1826 and 1836, Vol. III*, London, 1839. *The Structure and Distribution of Coral Reefs (Part I of the Geology of the Voyage of the 'Beagle')*, London, 1842. *Life and Letters of Charles Darwin*, ed. Francis Darwin London, 1887. *The Descent of Man and Selection in Relation to Sex*, London, 1888. *The Origin of Species*, London, 1888. *More letters of Charles Darwin*, ed. Francis Darwin and A. C. Seward, London, 1903. *The Voyage of the 'Beagle'*, London, 1906. *The Darwin Reader*, ed. Marston Bates and P. S. Humphrey, London, 1957. *The Autobiography of Charles Darwin, 1809–82*, ed. Nora Barlow, London, 1958. *The Voyage of the 'Beagle'*, ed. Millicent E. Selsam, New York, 1959. *Charles Darwin's Autobiography, with notes and letters depicting the growth of the 'Origin of Species'*, ed. Francis Darwin, New York, 1961.

Farrington, Benjamin *What Darwin really said*, London, 1966.

FitzRoy, Robert *Narrative of the Surveying Voyages of HMS 'Adventure' and 'Beagle' between 1826 and 1836, Vols. I & II*, London, 1839.

Grattan, C. Hartley *The Southwest Pacific to 1900*, Ann Arbor, 1963.

Huxley, Julian *The Living Thoughts of Darwin*, London, 1958. *Charles Darwin and his World* (with H. B. D. Kettlewell), London, 1965.

Irvine, William *Apes, Angels and Victorians : a joint biography of Darwin and Huxley*, London, 1955.

Lack, David *Darwin's Finches*, New York, 1947.

'Life' and Lincoln Barnett *The Wonders of Life on Earth*, New York, 1960.

Litchfield, H. E. *A Century of Family Letters 1792–1896*, London, 1915.

Mellersh, H. E. L. *Charles Darwin : Pioneer of the Theory of Evolution*, London, 1964. *FitzRoy of the 'Beagle'*, London, 1968.

Moore, Ruth *Evolution*, Morristown, N.J., 1964.

Wallace, Alfred Russel *Darwinism*, London, 1889.

West, Geoffrey *Charles Darwin, the fragmentary man*, London, 1937.

INDEX

Figures in **bold type** indicate pages carrying illustrations in colour; figures in *italic type* indicate pages carrying illustrations in black and white.